WHAT ARE THEY SAYING ABOUT
SEXUAL MORALITY?

What Are They Saying About Sexual Morality?

James P. Hanigan

PAULIST PRESS
New York/Ramsey

Library of Congress
Catalog Card Number: 82-80162

ISBN: 0-8091-2451-3

Published by Paulist Press
545 Island Road, Ramsey, N.J. 07446

Printed and bound in the
United States of America

Contents

Preface

In one of his most splendid books, concerned with the processes of changing religious understandings, Andrew Greeley noted that the question Christians asked about sexual morality, up until the 1960's, was, "How far can we go?" The answer generally given to such a question was "that you can't go very far at all."[1] Sexual expression was reserved for marriage, and even within marriage it was severely restricted and rarely discussed. In the short space of twenty years the answer has changed dramatically to suggest that you can go as far as you want. So complete has been this reversal of opinion, not only in secular writings but even in Christian literature, that Rustum and Della M. Roy, the authors of *Honest Sex,*[2] which they claim is "perhaps the most widely distributed book on *Christian sex ethics* ever printed," have recently affirmed that "every kind of sensual-sex experience can be legitimate, just as every kind of food may be eaten."[3]

This is certainly a change of monumental proportions in people's thinking, if not necessarily in their practice. It certainly represents a sexual revolution of one kind or another and, like all revolutions, has spawned a degree of chaos and confusion. The following pages will be concerned to trace the reasons for this revolution and to examine the rationales that have accompanied it, both those which have supported the change to one degree or another, and those which have tried to oppose the change. This book intends to show not only what they are saying about sexual morality, but, more importantly, why they are saying it.

1

In the first chapter, therefore, I will attempt to sketch the revolution in sexual morality[4] and to indicate some of the causes for it. I am concerned here to discover why theologians and ethicians thought it necessary to re-evaluate the more traditional position on sexual questions. Most readers will be familiar, at least in a general sense, with the social and economic factors that influenced changing moral perceptions. The growing concern with the prospect of overpopulation, the remarkable advances in medical technology which opened up new possibilities for controlling conception, a new affluence which produced heightened aspirations for personal fulfillment as reflected in the various liberation movements—all contributed greatly, if indirectly, to a new moral perspective on the meaning of human sexuality. Increasingly, sexuality came to be seen as a personal good rather than primarily as a social good. But there were also theological and ethical developments which provoked the crisis, and these will be the central concern of the opening chapter.

Crisis calls forth pastoral concern, and the Catholic Church was not remiss in replying to the crisis. Whatever evaluation one makes of the worth of the official response, several important documents[5] emerged from official Church circles. These documents sought to bring clarity and certainty to a confusing and uncertain situation. The most famous—or notorious—of these documents was, of course, the encyclical letter of Pope Paul VI, *Humanae Vitae*. Although the central purpose of this document was to deal with the birth control issue, the letter contains a rather comprehensive teaching on the purpose of human sexuality and its moral and immoral uses, and it deserves a wider and more careful reading than it is generally accorded. The second chapter, then, will give this attention to the official documents.

The encyclical itself provoked wide-ranging debate[6] and dissension which is still not at an end.[7] It was a debate that quickly went beyond the ban on artificial contraception to re-evaluate other prohibitions on sexual activity, most especially masturbation, homosexuality, and divorce and remarriage. This debate, especially on the dissenting side, will be the focus of Chapter 3. Interestingly enough, the debate took on ecumenical overtones, for if the papal position was not always persuasive, it was at least clear and so stimulated all Christians to clarify their own thinking and conclusions.

By the mid-1970's some of the opposition began to clarify itself sufficiently to make alternate proposals about a positive understanding of sexual morality in a wider context than the issue of artificial contraception. Much of the disagreement with the official position crystallized in the well-known study, *Human Sexuality,*[8] sponsored by The Catholic Theological Society of America. This work itself quickly became a cause for new discussion and debate.[9] Chapter 4 will investigate this development and other works of a similarly revisionist nature.

The official position of the Church has both its theological critics and theological champions. These writers do not restrict themselves to simple rejection or repetition of the papal position, but attempt to address that position in new, more carefully honed ways. Fairness and comprehensiveness require a consideration of the arguments of both critics and defenders of the official position. The fifth chapter will be given over to that consideration.

Finally a last chapter will take up the possibility of new directions for our understanding of human sexuality and morality. Pope John Paul II has been directing his Wednesday homilies to the understanding of bodily life based upon the creation stories in the Book of Genesis, seeking a more positive understanding of human sexuality. The 1980 Synod of Bishops, while upholding the Church's traditional teaching on specific sexual issues, did call for new, more pertinent ways of presenting and communicating that teaching. Theologians have not been idle in this regard either. If the new directions are not yet entirely clear, the materials are at hand for charting these new directions.

Christians, especially Catholic Christians in the United States and Ireland, have often been accused of being obsessed with sex and of equating morality with proper sexual conduct. The heritage of Puritanism and Jansenism are often blamed for this over-emphasis[10] and the resulting uncomfortableness with matter, the body, and all things sexual. However well- or ill-founded such accusations may be, human sexuality in its multiplicity of expressions has never been considered a trivial subject in the Christian tradition. While sex may indeed be fun, and often even funny, it is not a matter for mere jest and amusement. The amount of time and energy spent on determining a wise and faithful Christian sexuality testifies to the importance of the subject in Christian living. The debates about sexual morality are both serious and substantial. For ultimately sex and sexuality are only abstractions. The concrete reality is the sexed human being, male or female, made in the image and likeness of God. To trivialize sex, to make it a subject of jest or of little importance, is to cheapen the human person. What they are saying, then, about sexual morality is important, and it is in that conviction that this study is presented.

Notes

1. Andrew M. Greeley, *The New Agenda* (Garden City: Doubleday and Co., 1973), p. 132.

2. Rustum and Della M. Roy, *Honest Sex* (New York: New American Library, 1968).

3. "The Autonomy of Sensuality: The Final Solution of Sex Ethics," in Sol Gordon and Roger W. Libby (eds.), *Sexuality Today and Tomorrow* (North Scituate, Massachusetts: Duxbury Press, 1976), p. 322 (italics mine) and p. 327.

4. A useful introductory work on the sexual revolution is David R. Mace, *The Christian Response to the Sexual Revolution* (Nashville: Abingdon, 1970), esp. pp. 67–100. It does need to be used with care, especially in regard to generalizations about the Christian tradition.

5. The key documents to be discussed include Vatican Council II's *Pastoral Constitution on the Church in the Modern World* and Pope Paul VI, *Humanae Vitae,* both to be found in Joseph Gremillion, *The Gospel of Peace and Justice* (Maryknoll: Orbis Books, 1976), pp. 232–290 and 427–444; "Declaration on Certain Questions Concerning Sexual Ethics" (Dec. 29, 1975) to be found in Anthony Kosnik *et al.. Human Sexuality* (New York: Paulist Press, 1977), pp. 299–316; and several statements from the National Conference of Catholic Bishops (NCCB), to be noted when referred to in the text. A very useful compilation containing all the key documents is Odile M. Liebard (ed.), *Love and Sexuality: Official Catholic Teachings* (Wilmington, North Carolina: McGrath Publishing Company, 1978).

6. Useful summaries of this debate can be found in Charles

Curran *et al., Dissent in and for the Church: Theologians and Humanae Vitae* (New York: Sheed and Ward, 1969); William H. Shannon (ed.), *The Lively Debate: Response to Humanae Vitae* (New York: Sheed and Ward, 1970).

7. A recent effort to end the debate can be found in John H. Wright, "An End to the Birth Control Controversy?" *America* (3/7/81), pp. 175–178.

8. Anthony Kosnik *et al., Human Sexuality.*

9. This debate is available in Dennis Doherty (ed.), *New Dimensions in Human Sexuality* (Garden City: Doubleday, 1979).

10. See Philip S. Keane, S.S., *Sexual Morality: A Catholic Perspective* (New York: Paulist Press, 1977), pp. 7–8.

1
The Crisis in Sexual Morality

The word "crisis" is unquestionably overworked in our private and public rhetoric and yet there are times and situations for which crisis is the only correct word. These are times or situations in which decisions must be made, but those decisions are difficult because fraught with such serious consequences. The decisions to be made inescapably mark a turning point, inviting us to go in a new direction full of unknown possibilities or to forego forever those possibilities. People who are forced to make critical decisions do not always see at the time the crisis-nature of those decisions. Often it is only in retrospect that the critical quality of the decisions becomes clear.

The decision as to the moral acceptability of artificial contraception had this critical quality about it, though that was not always perceived to be the case.[1] And the widespread possibility of artificial contraception did indeed create a crisis in sexual morality, and not only in the Catholic Church.[2] For it struck at the fundamental guiding principle of Christian sexual morality, namely that the primary purpose or good of sexuality, as ordained by God, was the procreation and education of children. All sexual activity, from the initial rituals of dating and courtship to the full expression of sexual intercourse, was judged morally in the light of this primary end or good. It was realized, of course that sexuality served other purposes or goods. These were handily summarized as the mutual support of the

7

couple and as a remedy for concupiscence, but these purposes were clearly subordinated to the primary purpose of procreation.

The prospect of separating the procreation purpose of sexuality from its other purposes meant in fact that human beings could and would understand, experience and live their sexuality in new and different ways. Sexuality and sexual expression would take on new meanings, would have a different purpose, would seek to realize other goods. But should it? Was such a change in accord with the will of God? And could the Church, after all these centuries, change its teaching on so fundamental a matter?

The crisis in sexual morality, therefore, while focused on the specific issue of birth control, involved a great deal more than that one issue. It involved a whole host of issues which are worth noting at the outset of this study, for the subsequent discussions touch on all of them. Most clearly and immediately it raised anew the issue of the purpose of human sexuality and how human beings come to know this purpose. Was sex to be looked upon as something good in itself, or something granted to sinful beings as a concession to their weakness? What attitude should we adopt toward ourselves and one another as sexual beings? How do we evaluate our sexual behavior or come to know what is right and wrong sexually? Is it the province of the Church authority to dictate this or should it be left to a decision of the individual conscience? If the Church authority is to speak, does it do so in general terms—e.g., be faithful to your sexual partner—or in specific terms—e.g., it is always wrong to commit adultery? If the evaluation of sexual behavior is to be left to the individual conscience, what principles or methods can the individual person count on to guide his or her decisions? How does the individual avoid the rationalizations and self-deceptions to which all mortal flesh is prone?

The secular society had long since abandoned the Christian view of sexuality. Empirical studies like the two Kinsey Reports on male and female sexuality and the more recent Hite Reports[3] made it clear that the vast majority of people, at least in the United States, lived differently in their sexual lives than traditional Christian sexual morality proscribed. But that in itself posed little reason for Christians to change their own understanding of sexuality. Morality is not established by taking public opinion polls or by majority vote. There were, however, several reasons internal to Christian faith, as well as the external social and economic factors, that caused a crisis. These factors may be usefully discussed under the following headings: a new reading of Scripture; a more critical reading of the historical tradition; a new appreciation of the pertinence of psychological and sociological data; a renewed emphasis on love as the central ethical value in Christian life.

1. A New Reading of Scripture

As many authors have pointed out,[4] the New Testament, particularly in the four Gospels, has surprisingly little to say about sexual morality. The Old Testament is more specific in giving rules for certain practices, but there remain a whole host of specific sexual questions on which the Scriptures provide no direct and unambiguous answer. For the following sexual issues there is no scriptural text or story to which one can appeal with any certainty: masturbation, pornography, obscene jokes and language, nude bathing, nudist colonies, pre-marital sex, artificial contraception, male or female sterilization, artificial insemination, test-tube babies, and surrogate motherhood.[5] It is possible to find clear condemnations of freely chosen homosexual relations in both the Old and New Testaments,[6] but neither Testament shows any awareness of the condition of irreversible homosexual orientation. Both Testaments have condemnations of adultery,[7] but the reasons for the condemnations vary. The Synoptic Gospels all speak of Jesus' rejection of divorce and remarriage, but Matthew allows for an exception.[8] Paul, the most outspoken New Testament author on sexual morality, clearly rejects sexual relations with prostitutes, orgies, adultery, and voluntary homosexuality, and he favors celibacy over marriage. But he allows divorce and remarriage in one special case.[9] Nowhere does the New Testament even suggest that procreation is the purpose of sexuality and marriage.

While the conclusion of *Human Sexuality* on the biblical data to the effect that "critical biblical scholarship finds it impossible . . . to approve or reject categorically any particular sexual act outside of its contextual circumstances and intention"[10] may be too strong,[11] it is certain that no issue of sexual morality can be settled simply by quoting a text. But that does not mean that the revelation of God's word in Scripture leaves us without any help for working out a sexual morality. Three contributions in particular are worthy of note: the attitude toward sexuality; the purpose of sexuality; the importance of interior intentions in all sexual behavior.

Attitudes Toward Sexuality

The fundamental importance of attitudes in morality has been receiving increased emphasis in recent years,[12] yet it remains difficult to make a clear case for their practical importance. This is particularly true in regard to sexual morality where it is by no means easy for any person to distinguish psychological inhibitions from appropriate moral convictions. Yet one clear and consistent teaching of the Scriptures is that God created man male and female; he created sexual beings and sexuality, and when he looked at what he had made, he found it to be very good. Indeed, in the second creation story, the only thing not good is for the man to be alone, a situation quickly remedied by the creation of woman. For human beings to be is to be male and female. Sexuality is a part of God's good creation. It is not dirty, or an embarrassment, or a mistake. It is rather a gift and a blessing.[13]

It is not only the creation stories in the Book of Genesis that urge this positive attitude toward the fact of human sexuality. The entire Old Testament is replete with sexual imagery to describe the relationship between God and his chosen people, while the Song of Songs is an explicit hymn in praise of sexual attraction and love. This same attitude is reconfirmed in the Synoptic Gospels and nowhere is it contradicted in the New Testament except for a few passages in Paul, with which we will be concerned shortly. A careful, critical reading of the Scriptures has made it clear that the puritanical, Jansenistic and Victorian attitudes toward sexuality were mistaken ones, however common they may have been in the history of Christian faith. To be sure, both the Old and the New Testaments are well aware that sexuality, like all dimensions of human life, is disordered by sin and can be and often is misused.[14] But it still remains a great gift and blessing of God, to be rejoiced in and given thanks for.

While it may be easy to affirm and defend such a positive attitude toward sexuality, it is not so easy, as history testifies, to make it real in experience. As one eminent moral theologian has pointed out, the history of the Church reveals a propensity for sexual asceticism, even in marital relations. "This puritanical tendency infected Christian thinking from the late second century until shortly before Vatican Council II."[15] Even though Christian hostility toward the body, toward women, and toward all things sexual has often been exaggerated, there is no question that the perduring attitude toward sexuality has been and continues to be problematic and suspicious. Since this is so contradictory to the affirmative attitude of the Scriptures, it is important to ask why this has been the case.

On strictly internal Christian grounds, I would suggest two reasons. One reason is Paul's clear preference for celibacy over marriage, a preference as an ideal. This ideal has been institutionalized in the Church in the celibacy and virginity required of clergy and religious. The religious life has been thought of as a better or more excellent state of life. Intentionally or not, this preference for celibacy has tended to treat marriage as a second-class form of Christian life, a notion that is inescapably conveyed by Paul's dictum that it is better to marry than to burn. Almost from the outset, then, sexual morality takes on a negative cast, with the result that no positive and adequate theology of sexuality and marriage was developed.[16]

The second reason is the experience through history of the often unruly and disruptive nature of sexual attraction and sexual love. Sexual desire can and does cause problems, both personally and socially. Experientially sex is an ambiguous phenomenon. It is a source of both joy and sorrow, pleasure and pain, life and death, community and chaos. It draws some human beings away from God as readily as it draws others close to God. This ambiguity has marked the experience of many Christians who have put their stamp on the Christian tradition by the influence of their writings. Augustine is the most notable of such figures.[17] So sex is a reality that has caused people to be wary and to adopt an attitude toward sexuality that was rarely positive and clear. The central concern was not to experience the goodness of God's gift to the fullest, but to control its expression. As with all ambiguous realities, there is the tendency to move toward extremes—to adopt an attitude of extreme hostility or one of unfettered acceptance. This tendency toward extremes has marked the attitudinal history of the Christian tradition, if not the doctrinal history which has upheld the goodness and holiness of marriage.[18]

It is here where a new or renewed reading of the Scriptures is critical. For Paul's preference for celibacy, along with the Synoptics' praise for those who made themselves eunuchs,[19] urges two considerations to the forefront. It is not simply celibacy or virginity that is the ideal, but celibacy embraced for the sake of the kingdom of God. Both Paul and the Synoptic Gospels are clear that such a calling is not addressed to everyone and so does not constitute an ideal for everyone. Indeed, as several authors are again making clear,[20] marriage and consecrated celibacy need one another and enhance the value of one another. Where marriage is demeaned as a way of life, so also is the value of celibate commitment and sacrifice. Where the celibate commitment is demeaned, so also is the great human good of sexual love cheapened and trivialized.

The second consideration that arises from Paul's preference for celibacy for the sake of the kingdom is that there is something more important and more fundamental in human life for everyone than sexual fulfillment and the blessings of children and family. There is first the kingdom of God to which all other things are to be subordinated, sexuality and marriage included. A more concrete way of expressing the same idea is that the ultimate meaning of life is not to be found in sexuality. Sex is not the most important thing in human existence and is not to be turned into an idol, which is the temptation of modern culture. Yet, since it is in the service of the kingdom of God, sex is important and is not to be trivialized.

In practice, then, a careful reading of the Scriptures urges an attitude toward sexuality that perceives it as a basic human good, a great gift of God, but by no means the highest or ultimate good in which the very meaning of life is to be found. Sex is neither demonic nor divine. It is neither to be fled from nor worshiped, but turned to the service of God's kingdom. The implications of this attitude are important, but will be reserved for later discussion.

The Purpose of Sexuality

A second contribution that a critical reading of the Scriptures makes to the present re-evaluation of sexual morality has to do with the purpose of sexuality in human life.[21] It has been the express teaching of the Church from at least the time of Augustine up to the Second Vatican Council that the primary purpose of sexuality is the procreation of children. Sexuality was thought to serve a social good, the preservation of the species. That it also served other human goods was acknowledged, but these goods were considered to be secondary and subordinate to the good of procreation. This teaching, however, cannot be derived from a careful reading of the Scriptures. Neither the Synoptic Gospels which refer back to the Genesis accounts of creation nor the letters of Paul explain the meaning of sexuality in terms of procreation. They do not deny, of course, the procreative significance and importance of sexuality, but they do not appeal to it in explaining the purpose of sexuality. Rather the stress is on the human community of male and female that results from sexuality, the new two in one flesh reality that is formed when a man leaves his father and mother and clings to his wife. In the second creation account in Genesis, when God surveys his creative work before Eve has appeared on the scene, he finds one thing not good. It is not good for man to be alone. Only Eve is able to fill up Adam's loneliness, to be his partner and helpmate as he is to be for her. It is to the two becoming one that the Synoptic Gospels have Jesus appeal when explaining why God created them male and female.[22] Of course this union is given the command and the blessing to be fruitful and multiply. This union is to serve life; it does have procreative meaning. But that purpose is not mentioned as being the sole or even primary reason for the creation of man as male and female.

Paul is also of interest in this regard. He sees in the union of male and female a vehicle of mutual sanctification and a sign of the union of Christ with his Church.[23] To adopt a later terminology it is the unitive function of sexuality, not the procreative one, that is stressed in Scripture. It is the union, the two becoming one that the Bible proposes as the central purpose of sexuality, and it would seem, then, that that purpose must become the ruling norm for what is morally acceptable in sexual behavior.

This does not deny or overlook the high value given to procreation in the Scriptures. Children are clearly perceived to be a blessing and gift of God, the expected fruit of the sexual union. Female barrenness is looked upon as a curse and a humiliation—one need only think of Elizabeth, the mother of John the Baptist, on learning of her own pregnancy.[24] But child-bearing and rearing is not an obligation of nature in the Old Testament, but an obligation of the covenant. In the new covenant it is an obligation that may be overridden for the sake of the kingdom of God.

Interior Intentions

A third contribution to the re-evaluation of sexual morality is the radical stress that the gospel writers portray Jesus putting upon the intentions of the heart for a genuine morality.[25] This is not a new discovery, but it is receiving a renewed emphasis. How badly this emphasis is needed is reflected in the immediate sensation in the world press stirred up by Pope John Paul II's comment that "if a man gazes on his wife lustfully, he has already committed adultery with her in his heart." Marriage is not an excuse for wrong intentions. It is emphasized in Jesus' teaching that the most crucial element in morality is not the external act, but the inner intention from which the action proceeds. On what is a person's heart set? It is not what comes from without that corrupts us, but what proceeds from within. Calling one's brother a fool and lusting after a woman in one's heart are declared to be as morally corrupting as the external acts of murder and adultery.

The importance of intentions can also be highlighted in positive ways. Jesus' basic moral demand was a call for conversion.[26] What must we do to be saved? Repent and believe in the good news. The primary demand is not for a change in behavior but for a change of mind and heart. Turn away from intending the service of self and be intent upon seeking first the kingdom of God and the service of neighbor. In the Synoptics, in John's Gospel and First Epistle, and in Paul, love of God and neighbor exhaust and fulfill the whole law.[27] The essence of morality is found in what the heart loves, in what the human person interiorly intends. While love is not the only motive Jesus proposes for moral action, it is certainly the highest motive proposed to which all are invited to aspire.

This stress on interior intentions does not mean that external actions are without moral significance or that the real consequences of actions have no importance for morality. It is not a suggestion that morally it is enough simply to mean well or to have good intentions.[28] But it does indicate that the morality Jesus invited human beings to pursue cannot be confined within the limits of the written law.[29] No list or description of sexual acts, however long or exhaustive, can encompass the sexual morality of the Christian life. In practice this means that the Gospel morality demands personal responsibility for the conscientious decision of the individual.

2. The Historical Tradition

A second factor internal to Christian faith that helped precipitate the crisis in sexual morality was a more critical and adequate reading of the historical tradition. It may be that only those who were born and raised as Catholics can feel how important historical continuity in teaching and practice has been to the Church and how much authoritative weight is given to what has always been taught. From its beginnings the Church observed the principle of adhering to "what is believed everywhere, at all times by all."[30] The prospect of changing a teaching that was thought to have that kind of tradition behind it was almost unthinkable. In fact to some contemporary theologians[31] the weight of the historical tradition on the side of the immorality of artificial contraception gave that teaching the status of being infallible and so irreformable.

But critical historical studies have a way of showing that the tradition was often less uniform, less consistent and less certain than might appear to many in the present day. Studies by John Noonan on usury[32] and John Courtney Murray on religious freedom[33] have shown the pluralism in the historical tradition and have indicated the possibility of a change in the teaching on those matters. Studies by scholars like John Noonan on contraception,[34] John Connery on abortion[35] and John Boswell on homosexuality[36] show the pluralism in the tradition on sexual teaching. Such studies also reveal that some positions were adopted due to incomplete or inaccurate biological or psychological or philosophical knowledge, knowledge which is available to us today. Though it is not possible here to offer any kind of historical overview of the tradition on sexual morality,[37] three issues will serve to show how critical historical studies affected the crisis in sexual morality. These three issues are the role of woman, the behavior of animals and the knowledge of biology.

The Role of Woman

One of the most striking features of Philip Keane's recent book, *Sexual Morality: A Catholic Perspective,* and surely one of the signs of the times, is that it devotes an entire chapter to "The Role of Women as a Major Key in the Whole Picture of Human Sexuality."[38] Just how unprecedented and possibly even revolutionary such a step is can be appreciated only if one were to review historically past writings on sexual morality. Almost all were written by males for males and about males. As F. X. Murphy pointed out:

> A misogynistic (and patriarchal) prejudice has pervaded the Church's moral thought down through the ages, based on the incident of Eve as the temptress in Genesis, and confirmed by the Stoic rhetoric in which the early Christian thinkers were trained. It reflected the Platonic conviction that man's proper activity was contemplation. Churchmen from Tertullian and Cyprian in the third century to Jerome and John Chrysostom in the fifth delighted in denigrating womanhood as the source of the human race's downfall.
>
> While attributing mankind's woes to the lubricious enticements of woman, preachers with awe-inspiring inconsistency harped upon a wife's rendering the conjugal debt contracted in marriage by giving her husband the sole use of her body. That the contract worked both ways was also on the books, but little attention was paid to this consideration because it was taken for granted that the sex act had been created for the man's convenience.[39]

It is critical historical scholarship which has brought to light this misogynistic and patriarchal prejudice and which has shown how and why certain conclusions were reached about the morality of sexual conduct as a result of this prejudice. To give but one illustration, Cyprian insisted that virgins were obliged to dress with recognizable simplicity, avoid the arts of make-up, keep away from licentious wedding feasts and not go "to the baths where, even though she herself would remain pure when showing herself nude, she would be lusted after by men."[40] This might be good practical advice for a particular woman at a given time and place, but it hardly deserves classification as a moral teaching of lasting and authoritative merit.

The recognition of this prejudice in much of the tradition does not mean that the teachings received from the tradition are necessarily wrong, nor should it be an excuse for finding fault with our ancestors in the faith. What it does do at least is to call into serious question the received teachings for those who perceive that a woman is not an object of male sexual lust but an equal, active human subject. The obligation to safeguard the virtue of chastity is incumbent equally on men and women, nor can the meaning of chastity be different for men and women. This is a topic that is only just beginning to be explored,[41] and the implications of honoring the full human status of women are only slowly appearing. But the emergence of woman as a person in her own right is certainly fraught with consequences for sexual morality. One such consequence has already been recognized in law. It is possible, and now illegal, for a husband to rape his wife. Marriage may entail a right to the body of one's spouse, but it does not make the use of force right. It is possible, and morally wrong, as Pope John Paul II reminded us, for a husband to lust after his wife in his heart.

The emergence of woman as a fully responsible human person, however, also challenges the sexual morality of females. Her sexuality is not to be used as a weapon of seduction or manipulation, or as a reward and punishment mechanism designed to enable her to get her own way. It disparages the subtle, if unintentional, forms of sexual manipulation so warmly recommended in Marabel Morgan's popular book, *The Total Woman.*[42] The sexual relationship leading to the union of two in one flesh can only sustain its moral integrity if it is an equal and mutually caring relationship. It is time to stop talking about the obligation of a wife to submit to her husband's advances. Such an obligation, as Paul told the Corinthians,[43] can only be a mutual obligation.

The Behavior of Animals

One of the more persistent habits in the tradition of Western morality has been to equate what is immoral with what is unnatural. Such a habit is relatively harmless if we are clear as to what we mean by natural and unnatural and are on good grounds for how we know the difference. But historical studies have made it quite clear that that has not been the case in the Western tradition.[44] Contemporary students of animal behavior are not the first people who thought they could learn something about human nature by observing what animals do. Thomas Aquinas, for example, one of the most influential shapers of the Catholic moral tradition, was quite sure that anyone could discover what was natural—and so morally right—sexual behavior simply by observing what animals do.[45] Many of his conclusions in regard to sexual morality were based upon this conviction and upon what, apparently, he thought he observed.[46] Thomas was convinced, for example, that animals did not masturbate, did not engage in homosexual activity, and did not seek out species other than their own to satisfy their sexual instincts. Hence, he concluded that masturbating, homosexuality and bestiality were unnatural and so immoral.

In fairness to Aquinas it should be said that his argument about the unnaturalness of such activities is somewhat more sophisticated than as presented here. But once critical historical studies indicate the plurality of ways that nature is understood by Thomas and the basis on which his conclusions rest, those conclusions are called into serious question. For we have here two errors. Some animals do in fact do the things Aquinas said they did not do. His observations were either faulty or inadequate. If that is the case, perhaps his conclusions are also wrong. If homosexual activity is natural in the sense that some animals do engage in homosexual activity, is it, therefore, also morally right? More substantially, however, while human sexuality has points in common with animal sexuality, it is altogether different precisely because it is a human activity. It is an activity of conscious, free, rational persons which gives it a different meaning in every way. This point has been nicely illustrated by the eminent psychologist Rollo May in his observation that human beings are the only ones who engage in sex face to face.[47]

While it is true that we can learn many things by observing animals and the given principles of nature's operation, we cannot learn what is humanly right and wrong from such operation. If we are forced to alter Aquinas' understanding of the natural moral law,[48] are we also forced to alter his conclusions about sexual morality? In some ways it is clear that we are so forced. Aquinas ranked sexual sins in terms of their gravity according to whether they were more or less unnatural. In his ranking masturbation was judged to be a more serious sin than adultery or even rape. The use of artificial contraception was a more serious sin than fornication.[49] From any perspective of responsible behavior today, this ranking is certainly wrong. The crisis in sexual morality is heightened.

Knowledge of Biology

For most of the history of humankind, knowledge of the human reproductive system was seriously incomplete. The male seed was thought to contain the new human being and the female womb was regarded simply as the field in which the seed was planted and grew to ripeness. The male, therefore, had the active role in procreation just as he should have the active role in sexual intercourse. The female had an entirely passive role in procreation, as was also proper for her in the act of sexual intercourse. Infertility was a female problem, often regarded as a curse, and as more than adequate grounds for a divorce, as it still is in some places today.

Given this understanding of the procreative process, it is easy to see why artificial contraception, masturbation, *coitus interruptus* and abortion all had the same moral status, often being equated with murder.[50] It is easy to see why the primary purpose of sexuality was procreation, and why sexual intercourse during pregnancy was senseless and wrong, as well as after female menopause. Who plants a seed in a field that has already been planted or in a field known to be infertile?

With the discovery in the eighteenth century of the role of the female ovum in procreation, with the knowledge of the female menstrual cycle, with the realization that the male ejaculation in sexual intercourse hurls on the average 400,000 spermatozoa up the female vagina, any one of which is capable of fertilizing an egg and so creating a new human being—in short with the knowledge of modern biology—it is not even possible to think as our ancestors once thought. Who, today, could possibly accord masturbation and abortion the same moral status, even if one thinks that both are morally wrong? Once again, knowing how and why the historical tradition reached the conclusions it did about sexual morality forces us to question those conclusions and the teaching of the tradition. It does not, of course, necessarily force us to abandon the teaching, but it does cause a crisis in our understanding—either a new basis for the teaching must be found or the teaching must be changed.

3. The Social Sciences

At first glance it might be thought that the findings of the social sciences are not a factor internal to Christian faith but belong rather to the challenge presented to the faith by a changing secular culture. Understood in that way they should not impinge upon the crisis in sexual morality. Unfortunately, in some circles that seems to be the opinion so that there is little felt need to take these findings into account in working out a sexual morality. The Kinsey Reports, to take one example, might be interesting and informative as to what people actually do sexually, but they are irrelevant in determining what it is that people should do. Statistics are no basis for morality. To take a second example, it might be helpful from a practical point of view to know whether one out of five or ten or twenty people has a homosexual orientation, but that knowledge will not decide the question about the morality of homosexual behavior.

There is an obvious sense in which the above claims are quite true. The fact that something is the case does not mean necessarily that it ought to be the case. Something more than statistics is needed for morality. A deeper reflection, however, indicates that there is an intimate link between the findings of the empirical social sciences and the task of working out a Christian morality, particularly in regard to sexuality. For the Christian faith makes truth claims. And because it believes that truth is ultimately one since the author of all truth is one, it cannot afford to ignore truth from whatever sources truth may come. All students of human behavior, then, must be heard and evaluated, and sometimes when heard, they, too, precipitate the crisis in sexual morality. Two particular issues will serve to illustrate this claim: masturbation and homosexuality.

Masturbation

Masturbation, as a sexual practice, violates the traditional Christian understanding of the purpose of sexuality on two counts. For it serves neither a unitive function nor a procreative function in and of itself.[51] Its sole purpose is the pleasurable relief of sexual tension. As previously mentioned, Aquinas regarded it as a grave sin against nature, and it has generally been condemned in Christian morality as a seriously immoral practice. It has also generally been recognized in more recent times in pastoral practice and counseling as often a compulsive, not altogether free behavior, particularly on the part of teenage males, whose subjective culpability for the practice may at times be severely limited. But apart from these excusing circumstances, the teaching on masturbation as a sexual practice is that it is always morally wrong and in the Catholic tradition gravely sinful.

What, then, are we to think when we learn from statistical surveys of people's sexual practice that over ninety percent of American males engage in masturbatory activity at one time or another in their lives and that over forty percent of females also do, and the percentage is growing?[52] Do these statistics in any way bear on the morality of the practice or do they merely confirm a belief that we are all sinners and sin frequently in sexual matters? Do these statistics confirm the belief that our morality, especially in regard to sex, is at an all-time low, or do they suggest that the official teaching has misunderstood the purpose of masturbation in human life?

It is not to the point here to discuss what people are saying about the morality of masturbation. Nor is there any intention to suggest that the statistics alone—or any empirical findings—can settle the question of morality. The point to be made is that the knowledge derived from statistics like those on masturbation advances the crisis in sexual morality. For it forces very real questions upon us.

Can such a practice which is so common and which in many cases has no demonstrable unhappy consequences be as seriously wrong as has been traditionally taught? Since the teaching against masturbation certainly inculcates shame and negative sexual attitudes in a good number of people and at times causes a faith crisis for a considerable number of young people, perhaps it is incorrect or overly emphasized.

The reader will notice the tentative nature of those inquiries and how pastoral concern is joined with the ethical concern. The statistics will not answer such questions, but they do, inevitably and properly, force the moralist to raise them and so to enter upon a re-evaluation of the teaching on sexual morality.

Homosexuality

As with masturbation, so also with homosexuality, much of the contemporary concern is pastorally generated. What can be said about homosexuality to homosexuals that will be spiritually helpful and in keeping with Christian faith and morality? This time it is not statistics that raise questions but the discovery by psychological science of an apparently irreversible homosexual orientation whose cause is debated and still unknown. There is little doubt that homosexual acts are rigorously condemned in both the Old and New Testaments as unnatural and abominable in the sight of God.[53] The persistent teaching of the Christian churches has regarded homosexual behavior as immoral, since it clearly lacks any orientation to the good of procreation. But both the Scriptures and the tradition speak of homosexuality as a freely chosen way of behaving, and the persistent advice, even admonition, given by the churches to homosexuals was to change their behavior.[54]

If, however, it is the case that our sexual orientation is established long before the age of personal responsibility, and if in many cases this orientation is irreversible by any methods presently known to human beings, as modern psychology indicates, is it not clear that we are dealing with something rather different than what St. Paul condemned? If the only moral advice or counsel that can be given to homosexuals is to resign themselves to a life of perpetual celibacy and continence, how can we be so sure that we are right in our judgment about the moral quality of homosexual acts and relationships?

It needs to be emphasized once again that the fact of an irreversible homosexual orientation does not settle the moral question about behavior, any more than do statistics on the number of homosexuals in the population. But the examples of masturbation and homosexuality do illustrate how the findings of the social sciences raise real questions for the moralist and add to the crisis in sexual morality. Both fairness and compassion, basic Gospel virtues, insist that the moral question cannot be answered in ignorance or indifference to these facts.

4. The Centrality of Love

The fourth factor contributing to the crisis in sexual morality was the exuberant rediscovery of love as the central ethical value of Christian faith. This rediscovery was emphasized in scholarly works written in the 1950's. Notable among these works were Gerad Gilleman's *The Primacy of Love in Moral Theology,*[55] Bernard Häring's *The Law of Christ*[56] and Marc Oraison's *Love or Constraint.*[57] It was further popularized in the 1960's by John Robinson's *Honest to God,*[58] Harvey Cox's *The Secular City*[59] and Joseph Fletcher's *Situation Ethics,*[60] and people began to talk about "the new morality." These books were not exclusively or even primarily concerned with sexual morality, though they often used sexual issues and examples to illustrate their point. Nor were they all in agreement on specific issues by any means. But they did challenge the manner of doing ethics and articulating morality that took the form of enunciating rules and laws. Christian morality, they argued, is about loving God and one's neighbor. It is not about being obedient to rules and laws.

These works, and others that appeared in quick succession after them,[61] precipitated a crisis not only in sexual morality, but in the very meaning of morality itself and in the way ethics was done and expressed. It started a debate over the relative importance in Christian ethics of rules versus context or situation, a debate that was often misplaced, as James Gustafson pointed out in a classic essay.[62] Paralleling the appearance of the new morality in the Christian world was the growing popularity of the *Playboy* philosophy in the secular culture, a philosophy explicitly concerned with greater sexual freedom of expression and which declared any form of sexual behavior morally acceptable as long as no one got hurt. This slogan seems to bear a similar if somewhat pale resemblance to the slogan of the new morality to do the loving thing, and the crisis in sexual morality had reached its peak.

In its most extreme form, as articulated by Joseph Fletcher, love, and love alone, was the only thing that was always and absolutely good, and the Christian was charged in every situation with the single command to do the most loving thing. The way to decide what was the most loving thing to do in any particular situation was to weigh the foreseeable consequences of any proposed action and do that action which would bring about the best results for all concerned. It quickly became clear in this system of morality that anything might be permissible to love. It all depends on the situation. In time this conclusion was explicitly drawn. "Every kind of sensual-sex experience can be legitimate, just as every kind of food may be eaten."[63] The only limit to be put on sexual expression was that a person not coerce his or her sexual partner.

Not everyone who wished to embrace love as the central ethical value went that far in drawing conclusions. But most were willing to allow for greater sexual freedom than the traditional teaching had permitted. The first issue where this became evident was the ongoing debate over the morality of artificial contraception, a debate that quickly spread to other issues. And it was the birth control issue that sparked the first response from the official teaching office of the Church. So it is to that teaching we will turn in the next chapter.

Notes

1. Conservatives saw this more clearly than liberals, a point which Charles Curran makes in "Moral Theology in the Light of Reactions to *Humanae Vitae*," *Transition and Tradition in Moral Theology* (Notre Dame: University of Notre Dame Press, 1979), pp. 53–55.

2. John Noonan, *Contraception* (Cambridge, Massachusetts: Harvard University Press, 1965), p. 490, indicates the position of

many Protestant denominations and theologians on birth control and the dates on which they changed their positions.

3. Alfred Kinsey, Wardell Pomeroy and Clyde Martin, *Sexual Behavior in the Human Male* (Philadelphia, 1948); *Sexual Behavior in the Human Female* (Philadelphia, 1953); Shere Hite, *The Hite Report: A Nationwide Study of Female Sexuality* (New York: Dell Publishing Co., 1976); *A Nationwide Survey of Male Sexuality* (New York: Dell Publishing Co., 1981).

4. For example, Stephen Sapp, *Sexuality, the Bible, and Science* (Philadelphia: Fortress Press, 1977), p. 37.

5. I make no pretense that this list is complete.

6. Lev 20:13; Rom 1:27.

7. Lev 20:10; Mk 10:19.

8. Mk 10:1–12; Lk 18:10; Mt 19:9.

9. 1 Cor 7:15–16.

10. Kosnik *et al.,* p. 31.

11. John P. Meier, *The Vision of Matthew: Christ, Church, and Morality in the First Gospel* (New York: Paulist Press, 1979), pp. 1–2.

12. The emphasis centers around the discussion of a fundamental option or stance. A brief discussion can be found in George M. Regan, *New Trends in Moral Theology* (New York: Newman Press, 1971), pp. 189–208.

13. Useful discussions of the Genesis stories can be found in Pierre Grelot, *Man and Wife in Scripture* (New York: Herder and Herder, 1964), pp. 33–39; Sapp, pp. 1–21; Edward Schillebeeckx, *Marriage: Human Reality and Saving Mystery* (London: Sheed and Ward, 1965), pp. 8–89.

14. E.g., 2 Sam 12:1–15; 1 Cor 5:1–8.

15. Francis X. Murphy, C.SS.R., "Of Sex and the Catholic Church," *The Atlantic Monthly,* 247, 2 (February 1981), p. 44.

16. A recognition reflected at the 1980 Synod in Archbishop Bernardin's call for a more positive doctrine of sexuality.

17. John J. Hugo, *St. Augustine on Nature, Sex and Marriage* (Chicago: Scepter, 1969).

18. Kosnik *et al.,* pp. 33–52.

19. Mt 19:12.

20. See, e.g., the articles in *Spirituality and Sexuality: Studies in Formative Spirituality* II, 1 (February 1981), and George H. Frein

(ed.), *Celibacy: The Necessary Option* (New York: Herder and Herder, 1968).

21. The purpose referred to is not the conscious purpose of the subjects engaging in sexual activity, but the purpose intended by God, the objective purpose.

22. Mk 10:5–10.

23. 1 Cor 7:14–16; Eph 5:21–23.

24. Lk 1:25.

25. Mt 5:20–30; Mk 7:14–23.

26. Mk 1:15.

27. Jn 13:34–35; Jn 2:10; 1 Cor 13:1–13.

28. Stanley Hauerwas, "Love's Not All You Need," *Vision and Virtue* (Notre Dame: Fides/Claretian, 1974), pp. 111–126.

29. James T. Burtchaell, C.S.C., *Philemon's Problem* (Chicago: ACTA, 1973), pp. 58–65.

30. Murphy, p. 45.

31. John C. Ford, S.J. and Germain Grisez, "Contraception and Infallibility," *Theological Studies* 39, 2 (June 1978), pp. 258–312.

32. John T. Noonan, *The Scholastic Analysis of Usury* (Cambridge: Harvard University Press, 1957).

33. John Courtney Murray, S.J., "The Problem of Religious Freedom," *Theological Studies* 25, 3 (September 1964), pp. 503–575.

34. Noonan, *Contraception.*

35. John Connery, S.J., *Abortion: The Development of the Roman Catholic Perspective* (Chicago: Loyola University Press, 1977).

36. John Boswell, *Christianity, Social Tolerance, and Homosexuality* (Chicago: The University of Chicago Press, 1980).

37. A brief, popular presentation is Joseph Blenkinsopp, *Sexuality and the Christian Tradition* (Ohio: Pflaum Press, 1969).

38. Keane, pp. 20–34.

39. Murphy, p. 49.

40. Cited in George H. Tavard, *Woman in Christian Tradition* (Notre Dame: University of Notre Dame Press, 1973), p. 101.

41. For one example, Judith Plaskow, *Sex, Sin and Grace* (Lanham, Md: University Press of America, 1980).

42. Marabel Morgan, *The Total Woman* (London: Hodder and Stoughton, n.d.).

43. 1 Cor 7:4–5.

44. Boswell, pp. 145–156, 303–332.

45. *Summa Theologica,* II, II, q. 154.

46. *Ibid.;* see also I, II, q. 94.

47. Rollo May, *Love and Will* (New York: W. W. Norton and Company, Inc., 1969), p. 311.

48. Regan, pp. 115–142.

49. *Summa Theologica,* II, II, q. 154, a.12.

50. Noonan, *Contraception,* pp. 232–237.

51. Again it is the objective function that is meant, not the psychological purpose of the agents.

52. Hite, *Female Sexuality,* p. 591, estimates the number at 82 percent.

53. See note 16.

54. Robert W. Gleason and George Hagmaier, *Counselling the Catholic* (New York: Sheed and Ward, 1959), pp. 94–111.

55. Gerard Gilleman, *The Primacy of Charity in Moral Theology* (Westminster, Md: Newman Press, 1959).

56. Bernard Häring, *The Law of Christ,* I (Westminster, Md.: Newman Press, 1966).

57. Marc Oraison, *Love or Constraint* (New York: Paulist Press, 1961).

58. John A. T. Robinson, *Honest to God* (Philadelphia: Westminster Press, 1963).

59. Harvey Cox, *The Secular City* (New York: The Macmillan Company, 1965).

60. Joseph Fletcher, *Situation Ethics* (Philadelphia: Westminster Press, 1966).

61. Herbert McCabe, *What Is Ethics All About?* (Washington: Corpus Books, 1969); Charles E. Curran, *A New Look at Christian Morality* (Notre Dame: Fides, 1968); John Giles Milhaven, *Toward A New Catholic Morality* (Garden City: Doubleday and Co., Inc., 1970).

62. James M. Gustafson, "Context Versus Principles: A Misplaced Debate in Christian Ethics," *New Theology No. 3,* ed. by Martin E. Marty and Dean G. Peerman (New York: The Macmillan Company, 1966), pp. 69–102.

63. Roy and Roy, "The Autonomy of Sensuality," p. 327; authors' italics omitted.

2
The Response of the Church

On December 31, 1930 Pope Pius XI issued an encyclical letter on Christian marriage bearing the Latin title *Casti Connubii.* The occasion for the letter was the fiftieth anniversary of Pope Leo XIII's encyclical on Christian marriage, *Arcanum Divinae Sapientiae.*[1] These two papal encyclicals established the context and set the guidelines for future discussions of sexuality and sexual morality in the Catholic community. Two years before the publication of *Casti Connubii* the Anglican Church had relaxed its stand against contraceptive intercourse after a long period of struggle and debate.[2] Other Protestant denominations were to follow in steady succession.[3]

From the perspective of Pius XI the world presented a bleak picture. He saw the Church "standing erect in the midst of the moral ruin which surrounds her."[4] In writing his encyclical he saw it as his task to guard against what he called "these most pernicious errors and depraved morals" which were beginning "to spread even amongst the faithful and are gradually gaining ground."[5] In the letter he stressed that "amongst the blessings of marriage, the child holds the first place."[6] Accordingly he urged Christian parents to understand that it was their primary responsibility to produce children, not only for the preservation of the human species, but "children who are to become members of the Church of Christ, to raise up fellow-citizens of the saints, and members of God's household, that the worshipers of God and our Savior may daily increase."[7]

With that perspective on the world and marriage it came as no surprise that the Pontiff also condemned any act of contraceptive intercourse within marriage as "a deed which is shameful and intrinsically vicious," referring to Augustine's interpretation of the story of Onan for biblical confirmation of his position.[8] In the strongest and most unambiguous language he declared:

> Any use whatsoever of matrimony exercised in such a way that the act is deliberately frustrated in its natural power to generate life is an offense against the law of God and nature and those who indulge in such are branded with the guilt of grave sin.[9]

At the same time, however, the Pope left the way open to the method of birth control that came to be known as the rhythm method. It was not, he taught, against God's law or nature to engage in sexual intercourse even when natural reasons of time make conception impossible. For as Pius explained,

> In matrimony as well as in the use of the matrimonial rights there are also secondary ends, such as mutual aid, the cultivating of mutual love, and the quieting of concupiscence which husband and wife are not forbidden to consider so long as they are subordinated to the primary end and so long as the intrinsic nature of the act is preserved.[10]

In the teaching of both Leo XIII and Pius XI, sexuality finds its sole meaning in marriage, and so marriage is the central concept for their discussions. Marriage is understood to be of divine institution; consequently its structure, as monogamous and indissoluble, is not subject to human alteration. A person is in one of two states—married or not married. It is only the married person who is recognized as having any right to a sex life. All sexual activity outside the marriage relationship—pre-marital or extra-marital, heterosexual, homosexual or autosexual—and even some sexual activity within the relationship, is gravely sinful of its very nature. The unmarried person has the single choice of chastity, which then inevitably becomes understood as an essentially negative virtue. The chaste person is one who successfully avoids all deliberately willed venereal pleasure.[11]

Vatican II

The Second Vatican Council changed this essentially negative approach to sexuality, at least to a considerable degree, without changing the specific teachings in any substantial way. Since many theologians who are making new proposals in regard to sexual morality appeal to the teaching of the Council in support of their proposals, and because there is much debate over what the Council actually did teach, it seems necessary to support the claim that it made no substantial change in the teaching of Leo XIII and his successors. It will be helpful to do this first before looking at the very real changes the Council did effect.

Continuity with the Past

The central concern of the Council fathers in their teaching on sexual morality remains marriage and the family. They continue to regard marriage as of divine institution,[12] qualified by God's laws and, once entered into, no longer dependent on human decisions alone.[13] The marriage bond is effected by the mutual consent of the couple, a consent which they call personal and irrevocable,[14] a point Pope Paul VI highlighted in his address to the Sacred Roman Rota in 1976, urging greater rigor in the granting of annulments.[15] The Council fathers still see conjugal love and marriage by their very nature as "ordained for the procreation and education of children, and find in them their ultimate crown."[16] The marital union is thought to impose total fidelity upon the spouses and should never be profaned by either adultery or divorce.[17] Among the unmarried, only the young are singled out for consideration. "Young people should be instructed about the dignity, duty and expression of married love. Trained thus in the cultivation of chastity, they will be able at a suitable age to enter a marriage of their own after an honorable courtship."[18] Finally, although the Council fathers do not teach specifically on the morally acceptable methods of birth control, since Paul VI reserved that question to himself,[19] they do teach in general terms that the responsible limitation of children must be determined by objective standards, not merely by sincere intentions. Therefore the Council explicitly teaches:

> Sons of the Church may not undertake methods of regulating procreation which are found blameworthy by the teaching authority of the Church in its unfolding of the divine law.[20]

It did not say what methods are or should be considered blameworthy. Nor did it speak about the sexual life of unmarried adults.

These positions on sexual morality are in full continuity and harmony with the traditional teaching. What changes, then, did the Council effect in the area of sexual morality? In indicating these changes it may be helpful to draw an approximate parallel to the contributions a fresh reading of the Scriptures has made to sexual morality as discussed in the first chapter. In that way the changes effected by the Council can be conveniently treated under four headings: the attitude toward sexuality; the purpose of sexuality; the emphasis on personal conscience; the objective norm of morality.

Attitude Toward Sexuality

The attitude of the Council teachings in regard to human sexuality is most clearly revealed by contrasting it with other official statements, both prior to and after the Council. Leo XIII, for example, found himself in a situation where "the minds of many, being imbued with the opinions of a false philosophy and a corrupt habit of mind, bear nothing so ill as to submit and obey, and they labor with the greatest bitterness in order that not only individuals, but families, and indeed the whole human race, may profoundly despise the authority of God."[21] Pius XI, as mentioned, saw the Church "standing ... in the midst of moral ruin."[22] A later statement, the Vatican "Declaration on Certain Questions Concerning Sexual Ethics," begins by asserting that "in the present period, the corruption of morals has increased, and one of the most serious indications of this corruption is the unbridled exaltation of sex."[23]

In contrast to such a foreboding picture, the Council affirmed the longings of the world for greater freedom, identified with "the joy and hope, the grief and anguish of the man of our time," and lent its support to the quest for freedom and human dignity.[24] Following the open-window policy of Pope John XXIII, the Council opened itself to the world, not only to share its message of salvation with the world, but also in the desire to learn from and cooperate with all men in the building of a new humanism. The Council did not simply embrace the world uncritically, for it reminded that world of its sinfulness and brokenness, even in specific ways.[25] Yet it also recognized that a sinful, broken condition was the lot of the Church itself and that the Church, too, was in need of repentance.[26] In short, neither the tone nor the language of the conciliar documents is fearful and defensive.

Specifically in regard to sexuality, the Council stressed the intrinsic goodness of conjugal love, and the goodness of its sexual expression apart from any procreative purpose.

> The actions within marriage by which the couple are united intimately and chastely *are noble and worthy ones.* Expressed in a manner which is truly human, these actions signify and promote that mutual self-giving by which spouses enrich each other with a joyful and thankful will.[27]

It is a good thing, said the Council fathers, for the married couple to make love. The sexual expression of the couple's mutual love has a value apart from—but not unrelated to—the value of children. And the whole marital relationship "maintains its value and indissolubility, even when offspring are lacking. . . ."[28]

The Council did not fully explore the implications of this changed attitude toward the goodness of sexual love. Probably it was in no position to do so. Consequently some commentators on the conciliar teachings have been more impressed with the Council's continuity with the tradition in its explicit statements, while other commentators have seized upon this change in attitude as charting an almost revolutionary new direction. For such commentators the change in attitude bears a close parallel to the radical change of position the Council made on the right of religious liberty.[29] There was, however, at least one clear implication drawn by the Council from its changed attitude. That is to be seen in its teaching on the purpose of sexuality and marriage.

The Purpose of Sexuality

In harmony with the received tradition the Council taught explicitly that sexuality is ordered by God to conjugal love and that love in turn is ordered to the procreation and education of children.[30] But the Council refused to rank one purpose above the other, as had been traditionally done. Mutual love of the spouses, including the sexual expression of that love, was not subordinated to or judged less important or less good than the procreation of children. In contemporary terms the unitive and procreative functions of sexuality were accorded equal status. At the same time the Council insisted upon an inseparable link or unity between these two purposes. Sexual love, of its very nature, is intimately linked with the procreation of new life. Sexual love was declared to be both love-making and life-giving, but the Fathers refused to say that one was more important than the other.

Furthermore, showing a refreshing touch of realism, the Council recognized "that certain modern conditions often keep couples from arranging their married lives harmoniously, and that they find themselves in circumstances where at least temporarily the size of their family should not be increased."[31] These words, when taken seriously, are very significant. For they make two critical points. First, despite the inseparable link between the unitive and procreative functions of sexuality, as ordained by God, the conditions in which human beings live conspire at times to separate the two functions existentially, through no fault of the couple. A couple may want to make love and yet recognize that their family size ought not to be increased now. Conversely, though the Council did not deal with this side of the question, a couple may want to make life without making love (e.g., cases of artificial insemination by donor and surrogate motherhood). The recognition of this existential lack of harmony raises the question of the precise nature and importance of the inseparable link between the unitive and procreative functions of sexuality. Is it, perhaps, simply an ideal that cannot always be realized? Is it, perhaps, an ideal to be achieved in a total relationship and not in every specific act of sexual intercourse? How are we to explain our knowledge of and understanding of this inseparable link?

The second critical point in the above quotation is the explicit duty of responsible parenthood. The Council affirmed that at times family size ought not to be increased. This is affirmed not as a right, nor as a matter of preference or convenience, but as a duty. To have a child at this particular time because of these particular conditions would be an irresponsible act. It is something a couple ought not to do. Clearly, then, the Council is affirming the obligation of responsible parenthood in the context of family limitation. That obligation readily raises the question of what to do when a conflict of obligations arises. In the traditional, albeit unhappy, language of the Church's teaching on marriage, husband and wife contract a debt at marriage. They have the duty to submit their bodies to the exclusive use of their partners. That duty, to submit to the reasonable sexual advances of one's partner, and the duty not to have a child at this time, may well conflict. If the two ends of marriage are equal in status, if the two duties are equally binding, why should one take precedence over the other, as was the case when procreation was considered to be the primary end?

The Council's teaching on the purpose of sexuality, therefore, raised some difficult questions. Because it did not take up the birth control question explicitly, but only in general terms, the teaching quickly became a matter of debate and controversy that spread far beyond the one issue of birth control. It was as if the Council itself did not realize the full implications of its position on the purpose of sexuality.

Personal Conscience

One of the scriptural contributions to a renewed sexual morality was the Gospel stress on the importance of interior intentions to all moral behavior. The Council parallels this contribution by its stress on the dignity and importance of the individual conscience. "Conscience," the Council fathers declared, "is the most secret core and sanctuary of a man. There he is alone with God, whose voice echoes in his depths. In a wonderful manner conscience reveals that law which is fulfilled by love of God and neighbor."[32] This is not the place to expand on the Catholic understanding of conscience.[33] For present purposes it is sufficient to note the fundamental importance assigned to the individual conscience by the Council as the very seat of human dignity and to relate it to our topic. "Man's dignity . . . requires him to act out of conscious and free choice, as moved and drawn in a personal way from within, and not by blind impulses in himself or by mere external constraint."[34]

In the Council's discussion of responsible parenthood there is a continual insistence upon the importance of objective standards in the formation of conscience. The Council fathers were not hesitant in pointing out the kinds of objective considerations that a couple must weigh in determining the size of their family.[35] Nevertheless, the decision is finally left to the conscience of the couple. "The parents themselves should ultimately make this judgment, in the sight of God."[36] To this it is important to add the additional teaching that "conscience frequently errs from invincible ignorance without losing its dignity."[37]

Since it is possible to make both too much and too little of this teaching on conscience, a word of clarification is in order. The Council did not teach, and from a Catholic perspective it is hard to imagine that it ever could teach, that the morality of birth control or the morality of any sexual activity is simply to be left to the judgment of the individual conscience. In the Catholic view of things the authentic or integral conscience is inescapably ecclesial and social. To make decisions of conscience in indifference to or in spite of the Church's teaching is to forfeit one's claim to conscientiousness. On the other hand, in stressing the importance of the free, personal choice from within and in recognizing the possibility of conscience erring without losing its dignity, the Council breaks Catholic ethics out of the legalistic framework and gives it a more personalist orientation. In doing so it also establishes both the theoretical and practical grounds for conscientious dissent to official Church teachings. It is not surprising, therefore, that many of the early responses to *Humanae Vitae* were concerned, not with sexual morality as such, but with the issue of the relationship of conscience to official teaching (to the magisterium).[38]

The Objective Norm of Morality

Since the Council clearly stressed the importance of objective criteria for an adequate sexual morality, where are these criteria to be found? From whence are they to be drawn? The Catholic tradition has long called upon human nature as a fundamental criterion or standard for judging the morality of any action. An action that is in accord with nature is moral. An action which contradicts nature is both unnatural and immoral. But, as pointed out earlier,[39] it is hard to find one consistent and clear understanding of human nature. In urging the importance of objective standards, the Council taught that they were "based on the nature of the human person and his acts."[40] This basic norm was quickly taken up and employed in diverse ways to different purposes.[41] It is here where the disputes about sexual morality are most sharply engaged. For how are we to understand the nature of the human person and his or her acts? What is the normatively human?

The change represented by the Council's teaching is to be found in its language. It is not human nature that is proposed as the source of objective criteria but the nature of the human person and his or her acts. To the unwary reader the change may seem to be merely a verbal one. But it is not.[42] The difference may be indicated briefly here, since it will be a continuous source of concern throughout the rest of this study. It has long been a staple of popular wisdom that human nature never changes. Whether that nugget of wisdom is true or false, it is also a popular conviction that human persons change. Persons grow, develop, gain new insight, make new choices, and can be a constant source of surprise and wonder. If objective standards are based upon human nature, they might not be expected to change over time. But if they are based upon the nature of the human person, they might well be expected to change with different times and circumstances. Once again the Council teaching gives rise to questions and controversy. The most immediate controversy was the one about birth control which Paul VI attempted to resolve with the publication of *Humanae Vitae* in 1968. It is to that letter, therefore, that we next turn.

Humanae Vitae

Although the primary concern of *Humanae Vitae* was with the specific issue of birth control, the letter attempted to approach the issue from a larger context. As the Pope himself expressed it, "every . . . problem regarding human life is to be considered . . . in the light of an integral vision of man and of his vocation, not only his natural and earthly, but also his supernatural and eternal vocation."[43] Therefore, the letter has implications for sexual morality beyond the single issue of birth control.

Borrowing explicitly from the teachings of the Second Vatican Council which have just been discussed, Paul insisted that conjugal love is a gift of God, and it is one way in which God realizes his design of love for mankind. This gift leads husband and wife toward a communion of their beings whose purpose is the mutual perfection of one another and the collaboration with God in the generation and education of new children of God. In short, he taught once again the inseparable link between the unitive and procreative ends of marriage. Furthermore it is conjugal love itself which demands responsible parenthood of the couple, for this gift of God is to be used in neither an inhuman nor a careless manner. Once again responsible parenthood is proclaimed to be a duty demanded by love.[44]

The meaning of responsible parenthood as the fundamental mission of the married couple can be spelled out in a number of basic conditions. It requires, first of all, a knowledge of and respect for the biological processes and functions of human persons, clearly a demand originating in the goodness of God's creation. Second, it calls for the domination of the tendencies of instinct or passion by human reason and will. Human sexuality is not animal sexuality, and so can never be properly merely instinctual; it must also be free and reasonable. Third, responsible parenthood demands a consideration of the physical, economic, psychological and social conditions of life from which the couple will draw reasons for or against increasing family size. Finally, responsible parenthood calls for a recognition of what the couple's duties are toward God, toward themselves, toward the other members of the family and toward society as a whole.[45] These conditions make clear that the couple is not morally free to do whatever they please in regard to new life, but must honor the objective conditions of existence which ultimately are rooted in God's creative and redemptive activity.

The crucial point of the papal discussion, however, always returns to "the inseparable connection, willed by God and unable to be broken by man on his own initiative, between the two meanings of the conjugal act: the unitive meaning and the procreative meaning."[46] It is only by safeguarding both meanings that the very nature of man and woman and their relationship can be respected, and so the plan of God can be respected.[47] On this basis the Pope enunciates a clear and unequivocal teaching: "Each and every marriage act must remain open to the transmission of life."[48] Nor is he hesitant in drawing further conclusions. Not only the use of artificial contraceptives is excluded, but also direct abortion, direct sterilization, and anything else before, during or after sex which would make conception impossible.[49] For, "just as man does not have unlimited dominion over his body in general, so also, with particular reason, he has no such dominion over his generative faculties as such, because of their intrinsic ordination toward raising up life, of which God is the principle."[50]

If pressed to answer how he knows that this is, in fact, God's will, the Pope has appealed to three considerations, the most fundamental of which is "the very nature of marriage and its acts,"[51] which is an argument from natural law. He also appeals to the constant teaching of the Church[52] and to the consequences that result from the use of methods of artificial birth control.[53] Among such consequences he foresaw an impetus to conjugal infidelity, a lowering of moral standards in general, and a loss of respect for women "to the point of considering her as a mere instrument of selfish enjoyment, and no longer as his respected and beloved companion."[54] He also foresaw the unwarranted intrusion of the state into the most personal and most reserved sector of conjugal intimacy. He was to find himself disputed on all three grounds.

Finally, by way of a pastoral appeal and exhortation, Pope Paul tried to indicate what would be required to live his proposed morality, the benefits that would be reaped from it, and the spiritual helps available to those who found it difficult or even in their weakness failed to live it. Two qualities are emphasized as essential for the couple: "solid convictions concerning the true values of life and of the family" and ascetical practices that enable reason and will to dominate the instinctual life. In turn, the Pope contends, these qualities enhance mutual love by driving out selfishness and deepening a sense of responsibility. This enables the parents to have greater influence on their children and bestows the fruits of serenity and peace on the family.[55] Admitting that the way of life is not easy because of sin and human weakness, the Pope recommends prayer, the sacraments, especially the Eucharist, the pastoral compassion of priests and the help of other married couples.

At the heart of the matter there would seem to be two essential concerns about sexual morality, concerns which are very much related to the double function or meaning of sexual intercourse. One concern is to protect and enhance the good of human life in its sheer givenness or facticity. That is to say, there is a clear perception of the very being of the human as good, as coming from the hands of God and destined to return to him. The papal concern in the encyclical is not primarily with the quality of human life or with the essential material conditions in which life is lived.[56] He is clearly disturbed by what has come to be called the contraceptive mentality, a mentality which closes itself off to the creation of new life and which sees newborn children not as a gift and blessing but as an imposition or inconvenience. Since sexuality seems clearly intended by God to be at the service of human life, he finds in all uses of artificial contraceptives a frustration of that purpose and a turning away from the goodness of life. Nor is he content to simply condemn the mentality. He finds every sexual act not open in principle to the gift of new life to be seriously disordered. While he makes a conscious effort to adopt the personalist approach of the Council to sexual morality,[57] he continues to find morally normative the biological processes and laws of the human condition.

The second concern is to keep human the instinctual basis of sexuality, a concern which is reflected in the repeated demand for the control of instinct or passion by reason and will. It is reflected in the warnings against "sense excitation and unbridled customs,"[58] against sexual license and "licentious performances." It is, perhaps, most clearly reflected in the subtly stated conviction that the desire of a husband and wife for one another is a weakness, which needs to be disciplined and brought under control.[59]

Other Documents

With the publication of *Humanae Vitae,* the public debate was on. Bishops' conferences found it necessary to add their voices either to support the papal teaching or to clarify the rights of conscience,[60] and the Vatican found it necessary to intervene as the debate extended to other moral issues. The American bishops have issued two documents worthy of notice,[61] and we will consider them briefly here before turning to a consideration of the more recent Vatican Declaration on Sexual Ethics. In November 1968, the National Conference of Catholic Bishops issued a pastoral letter, *Human Life in Our Day,* as their comment upon the Pope's encyclical. Eight years later another pastoral letter appeared entitled *To Live in Christ Jesus* whose subtitle described it as "A Pastoral Reflection on the Moral Life." As one student of the bishops' statements has put it, "in both pastoral letters . . . the American bishops clearly express their opposition to contraception. They strongly support Pope Paul; they add nothing new to his reasoning as presented in *Humanae Vitae* but simply repeat that position. And . . . there is extensive emphasis on authority."[62]

Yet the American bishops do make some points of their own that are of interest. Their main concern is with the condition of the family and what they call its "prophetic mission, a witness to the primacy of life and the importance of whatever preserves life."[63] This prophetic witness is seen in the family in terms both of its fidelity to life now and its hope for the future of life. Therefore, argue the bishops, "in its emphasis on the virtues of fidelity and hope . . . Christian sexual morality derives . . . not from the inviolability of generative biology, but ultimately from the sanctity of life itself and the nobility of human sexuality."[64] The openness to life of marital sexuality is seen as openness to God. The fidelity to love in marriage is seen as fidelity to God.

Furthermore, they find hope and fidelity to be gravely imperiled whenever the family is looked on as an instrument of pleasure or convenience for its individual members or as a means of economic or political advantage. In an eloquent passage the bishops state their understanding of family.

> For the believer, the family is the place where God's image is reproduced in his creation. The family is the community within which the person is realized, the place where all our hopes for the future of the person are nourished. The family is a learning experience in which fidelity is fostered, hope imparted and life honored; it thus increases the moral resources of our culture and, more importantly, of the person. The family is a sign to all mankind of fidelity to life and of hope in the future which become possible when persons are in communion with one another; it is a sign to believers of the depth of this fidelity and this hope when these center on God; it is a sign to Christians of the fidelity and hope which Christ communicates as the elder brother of the family of the Church for which he died.[65]

In the bishops' understanding of sexual morality, then, the virtues of hope and fidelity come to the fore. The proper use of one's sexual powers proceeds out of these virtues and should foster and enhance these virtues. Unfortunately, in repeating the papal ban on contraception, they do not show how or why the prohibition follows upon or flows from the virtues of fidelity and hope.

The "Declaration on Certain Questions Concerning Sexual Ethics" put out by the Sacred Congregation for the Doctrine of the Faith was published at the end of December 1975. It was occasioned by what it saw as a "confusion of minds and relaxation of morals." It broke no new ground, nor was that its intention. Rather it sought "to repeat the Church's doctrine on certain particular points, in view of the urgent need to oppose serious errors and widespread aberrant modes of behavior."[66] While admitting the profound importance of sexuality to the human person, the Declaration was more concerned with "the unbridled exaltation of sex" and "licentious hedonism."

The Declaration took as its starting point what it judged to be demanded by the dignity and vocation of the human person. Human dignity requires that people "discover, by the light of their own intelligence, the values innate in their nature, that they should ceaselessly develop these values and realize them in their lives, in order to achieve an even greater development.[67] Human dignity means that the essential order of human nature is to be respected. When human beings enter upon this journey of discovery they find that both divine revelation and philosophical wisdom point to genuine needs of human nature. In turn these authentic needs "manifest the existence of immutable laws inscribed in the constitutive elements of human nature and which are revealed to be identical in all beings endowed with reason."[68]

When one focuses on human sexual nature, the result is the same. "Principles and criteria which concerned human sexuality" are discovered "which are based upon the finality of the specific function of sexuality"; "it is respect for [this] finality that ensures the moral goodness of this act."[69] Following the Second Vatican Council, the Declaration asserts this finality of the function of sexuality to be mutual self-giving and procreation. On the basis of this theoretical structure, the Declaration goes on to condemn all pre-marital sex— "every genital act must be within the framework of marriage"—all living-together arrangements of male and female that omit a publicly valid marriage, all homosexual acts, all masturbatory acts which are further declared to be "intrinsically and seriously disordered."[70]

The Declaration expresses two other major concerns. The first is to repudiate the notion that sexual sins are rarely if ever serious or mortal. While conceeding that sexual sins, because of their nature, might at times be less than serious due to a diminished consent, such diminished consent ought not to be lightly presumed. This is true even about such a common practice as teenage masturbation. Passion, immaturity, habit, and psychological imbalance can all diminish the deliberate character of sexual activity and so diminish subjective culpability. But neither should the moral capacity of people be misunderstood or downplayed. Therefore, the Declaration insists, "according to Christian tradition and the Church's teaching, and as right reason also recognizes, the moral order of sexuality involves such high values of human life that every direct violation of this order is objectively serious."[71]

The second concern of the Declaration is to promote the virtue of chastity, a virtue which "is in no way confined solely to avoiding the faults already listed."[72] As the Declaration understands it, chastity has both an interior and an exterior dimension. In its exterior dimension what counts as chaste behavior is relative to one's state in life. One form of behavior is proper to the life of consecrated celibacy and virginity, another to the married life, still another to the single life. Unfortunately the Declaration does not say anything concrete about what is proper to the single life or to the celibate life. Such directives for behavior as there are essentially are negative, implying that only the married are to have any sex-life. In its internal dimension, chastity means the pure heart that does not lust. It is described as a kind of spiritual instinct that gives insight into what chastity demands. Perhaps most fundamentally, the virtue of chastity is understood as an empowerment or enablement. While it does not "suppress the concupiscence deriving from original sin, nor the promptings to evil in this world,"[73] it does enable the person to overcome temptation. More positively it enables the human person "to love truly, disinterestedly, unselfishly and with respect for others."[74] In sum, chastity seems to be that virtue which enables the human person to control the power of *eros* and integrate it with and in the interests of *agape.*[75]

This review of what official Church teaching has been saying about sexual morality is representative rather than exhaustive. It does make clear certain basic themes, methods, and specific concerns. The double finality of sexuality is one persistent theme as is the total ignoring of the place of pleasure in sexual expression. The method of ethical analysis employed is consistently a natural law methodology, buttressed by appeals to scriptural texts. The specific concerns for the goodness of life and for the discipline and control of sexual desire are likewise constant. It is hard to escape the impression that the official teaching, while it may see sex as God's gift to human beings, certainly regards sex as dangerous. Be that as it may, it is the official teaching that serves as the foil for making other proposals and saying other things about sexual morality. These alternatives began to be voiced in regard to birth control. Therefore we begin the next chapter by turning to that controversy.

Notes

1. Both letters can be found in the collection edited by Liebard, pp. 1–22, 23–70; citations will be from this edition.

2. The statement of the Lambeth Conference can be found in Kosnik, p. 45.

3. Noonan, *Contraception,* p. 490.

4. *Casti Connubii,* 82, p. 41.

5. *Ibid.,* 29, p. 24.

6. *Ibid.,* 37, p. 27.

7. *Ibid.,* 39, p. 27.

8. *Ibid.,* 80, p. 41.

9. *Ibid.,* 82, p. 41.

10. *Ibid.,* 85, p. 42.

11. Liebard, "Introduction," p. xx.

12. It is important to note the expression "of divine institution." Marriage is not a divine institution, but a human reality. The teaching is that it was instituted by God for human beings.

13. The Council's teachings on marriage are to be found in *Gaudium et Spes: Pastoral Constitution on the Church in the Modern World,* published December 7, 1965, 47–52; the document itself is cited from Walter M. Abbott, S.J. (ed.), *The Documents of Vatican II* (New York: Guild Press, 1966), pp. 249–258. The reference in the text is to 48, p. 250.

14. *Ibid.*

15. "Address of Pope Paul VI to the Sacred Roman Rota," Liebard, 1601, p. 452, and 1607, p. 454.

16. *Gaudium et Spes,* 48, p. 250.

17. *Ibid.,* 49, p. 253.

18. *Ibid.*

19. *Ibid.,* nn. 172–173, p. 256.

20. *Ibid.,* 51, p. 256.

21. "Arcanum Divinae Sapientiae," 8, p. 8.

22. See note 4.

23. "Declaration on Certain Questions Concerning Sexual Ethics," Liebard, 1519, p. 429, Kosnik, 1, 299.

24. *Gaudium et Spes,* 1–16, pp. 199–215.

25. See *ibid.,* 4, pp. 201–203; 8, pp. 205–206; 19–20, pp. 215–

218; 37, pp. 234–235; for specific condemnations, 66, pp. 274–275; 79–83, pp. 291–298.

26. *Ibid.,* 21, pp. 218–220; *Dignitatis Humanae,* 1, p. 677 and n. 4; *Unitatis Redintegratio,* 3, p. 345; *Nostra Aetate,* 4, p. 666.

27. *Gaudium et Spes,* 49, p. 253.

28. *Ibid.,* 50, p. 255.

29. See *Dignitatis Humanae,* pp. 675–696, and Charles E. Curran, *Ongoing Revision in Moral Theology* (Notre Dame: Fides/Claretian, 1975), pp. 76–77.

30. *Gaudium et Spes,* 48, p. 250.

31. *Ibid.,* 51, p. 255.

32. *Ibid.,* 16, p. 213.

33. See Regan, pp. 145–185.

34. *Gaudium et Spes,* 17; the translation in the text is from Austin Flannery, O.P. (ed.), *Vatican Council II: The Conciliar and Post-Conciliar Documents* (Collegeville: The Liturgical Press, 1975), p. 917.

35. *Gaudium et Spes,* 50, p. 254.

36. *Ibid.*

37. *Ibid.,* 16, p. 214.

38. See preface, note 6.

39. See Chapter 1, note 54.

40. *Gaudium et Spes,* 51, p. 256.

41. See the use made of this in Kosnik, p. 90 and the Vatican, Kosnik, pp. 302–303.

42. *Ibid.,* pp. 38–91.

43. *Humanae Vitae,* cited from Liebard, 7, p. 334.

44. *Ibid.,* 10, p. 335.

45. *Ibid.,* 10, pp. 335–336.

46. *Ibid.,* 12, p. 336.

47. *Ibid.,* 13, p. 337.

48. *Ibid.,* 11, p. 336.

49. *Ibid.,* 14, pp. 337–338.

50. *Ibid.,* 13, p. 337.

51. *Ibid.,* 10, p. 336.

52. *Ibid.;* see also *Gaudium et Spes,* 51, note 173, p. 256.

53. *Humanae Vitae,* 17, p. 339.

54. *Ibid.,* 17, p. 340.

55. *Ibid.,* 21, p. 342.

56. Paul VI was neither oblivious of nor indifferent to such concerns, even in *Humanae Vitae,* e.g., 23, p. 343. Those concerns are treated, however, in other letters, especially *Populorum Progressio,* Gremillion, pp. 387–415.

57. "Address of Pope Paul VI to a General Audience, July 31, 1968," Liebard, 1238, p. 351.

58. *Humanae Vitae,* 22, p. 342.

59. *Ibid.,* 29, p. 346.

60. Some of the episcopal statements are discussed in Richard A. McCormick, "Notes on Moral Theology, January–June 1969," *Theological Studies* 30, 4 (December 1969), pp. 635–668. A severe, and I think unfair, criticism of McCormick is William B. Smith, "The Revision of Moral Theology in Richard A. McCormick," *Homiletic and Pastoral Review* (March 1981), pp. 8–28.

61. National Conference of Catholic Bishops, *Human Life in Our Day* (Washington, D.C.: USCC Publications Office, 1968); *To Live in Christ Jesus* (Washington, D.C.: USCC Publications Office, 1976). Citations will be from Liebard's text.

62. Kenneth R. Overberg, *An Inconsistent Ethic?: Teachings of the American Catholic Bishops* (Lanham, Md.: University Press of America, 1980), p. 81.

63. *Human Life in Our Day,* 1259, p. 357.

64. *Ibid.,* 1260, p. 357.

65. *Ibid.,* 1257, pp. 356–357.

66. "Declaration," Kosnik, 6, p. 303.

67. *Ibid.,* 3, p. 300.

68. *Ibid.,* 4, p. 301.

69. *Ibid.,* 8, pp. 302–303.

70. *Ibid.,* 10, p. 308.

71. *Ibid.*

72. *Ibid.,* 12, p. 312.

73. *Ibid.,* 12, p. 311; chastity is discussed in paragraphs 11–13, pp. 309–313.

74. *Ibid.,* 12, p. 312.

75. For a good discussion of the possibility of such integration see John Giles Milhaven, "Response to 'Pure Love' by Robert Merrihew Adams," *The Journal of Religious Ethics* 8, 1 (Spring 1980), pp. 101–104.

3
The Birth Control Controversy

The groundwork for dissenting views on *Humanae Vitae* had been laid long before the actual publication of the encyclical itself. Vigorous debate about the morality of various contraceptive and sterilizing procedures had been carried on in the international theological community for years.[1] The debate had come to a head, as it were, in the papal study commission on birth control appointed by John XXIII and enlarged by Paul VI.[2] In submitting its report, the commission found itself divided. A substantial majority recommended a change in the traditional teaching prohibiting all artificial methods of contraception, while a minority argued in favor of adhering to the traditional prohibition.[3] Many of the points in the dispute had nothing to do with sexual morality as such. There was debate over the authority to be accorded to the tradition and to papal teachings in particular, over the place of public opinion in the Church (the *consensus fidelium*), over the possibility of a development in doctrine, or, more radically still, a change of doctrine. Adherence to the official teaching on birth control and to the practices it prescribed was seen by some not as a matter of sexual morality so much as a test of institutional loyalty and obedience to papal authority.[4]

Nevertheless, the central question was not altogether lost sight of—What constitutes a responsible Christian use of sexuality in marriage?—and, secondly: What are the proper grounds or warrants for the answer to that question? The advocates of change had particular difficulty with the second question because two of the classical sources of theological evidence seemed to be against them. The historical tradition and the teaching of the official magisterium were almost painfully clear; contraceptive intercourse was an intrinsically disordered action. So clear did this seem to some theologians, in fact, that change was all but incomprehensible. Writing in the *New Catholic Encyclopedia* on the morality of contraception, Joseph Farraher, for one example, declared:

> It has been the constant teaching of the Church through all ages that deliberate contraception between husband and wife is always intrinsically wrong and against the law of God and nature. This has been such a constant teaching, as something that must be accepted by all Christians, that it can be said to be guaranteed by the infallibility of the Church.[5]

To advocate a change, therefore, seemed to require the proponents of change to show how their new proposal was, in fact, in harmony with the received tradition and even demanded by it in the light of the new circumstances of the modern world. The papal commission on birth control attempted to do just that and so left a basic resource document for later dissenters to *Humanae Vitae.* It will be useful to examine the reports of the commission[6] as providing a framework for later discussion. In doing this we will be especially concerned with the understanding of sexuality and morality that the reports evidence.

The Birth Control Commission

The argument for a change in the teaching about the majority of contraceptive intercourse proposed by the majority of the papal commission on birth control can be outlined in four steps. The first step is to express agreement and continuity in fundamental principles and values associated with marital sexuality. A second step calls for an understanding of responsible parenthood in which the proposed change is included. The third step requires a demonstration of how this change is really a development of traditional teaching called for by modern conditions. The final step is to show how the new position is to be objectively applied in practice. These four steps provide a useful outline for the rest of this chapter.

1. Fundamental Values[7]

At the outset of the discussion on sexual morality in the Christian context there is widespread agreement[8] that sexuality, as created and ordered by God, is intended to lead human beings into that community of life and love known as the family. Nor is there any dispute about the central importance of the family to the well-being of individuals and society in general.[9] Sexual attraction and sexual desires are designed to lead to a true conjugal union of persons, or, in simpler language, they find their true fulfillment and meaning in the personal relationship of marriage. This relationship called marriage has as its distinctive characteristic the total, mutual self-giving of spouse to spouse. The giving of self in sexual intercourse is both an expression and a realization of this total, mutual self-giving, though it surely does not exhaust the meaning of self-giving. The aim or goal of mutual self-giving is the mutual perfection of the partners and the formation of a true community of life and love. Consequently there is no dispute that mutual fidelity and indissolubility ought to be basic characteristics of this relationship. Or, as the sacramental sign of Christ's union with his Church, the marital relationship should be marked by an always faithful, never-dying love, as the Church has always taught.

There is a further common recognition that this conjugal love which marks the relationship called marriage will not be authentic if it is not also fruitful in bringing forth new life, the clearest sign of which is the birth of children. As the papal commission asserted, "Conjugal love and fecundity are in no way opposed, but complement one another in such a way that they constitute an almost indivisible unity."[10] Therefore conjugal love clearly excludes an egoistic union in which the partners seek only themselves as well as a union whose main intent is hedonistic self-gratification. Conjugal love, if authentic, is also seen to demand the virtue of chastity and to require the guidance, not of the arbitrary whims of the couple, but of the laws of God and nature.

> Consequently an egoistical, hedonistic and contraceptive approach, which arbitrarily turns the practice of married life away from its ordination to a human, generous and prudent fecundity is always against the nature of man and can never be justified.[11]

In its general expression this understanding of marital sexuality and morality is indisputably in accord with the Christian tradition. The love of the couple is made the focal point of the discussion, and this has continued to be the case. As Charles Curran has pointed out, "Generally all Christian ethicists today, Protestant and Roman Catholic, view human sexuality in terms of a personal relationship between man and woman. Sexuality is not a mere object or even a faculty divorced from the person, but a very personal and intimate way of woman and man giving themselves to one another in a relationship of love."[12] Sexual expression finds its primary meaning as an expression of love, a love that needs marriage and children for it to be authentic and responsible. Sexual intercourse does not have as its primary justification the procreation of children, but the bonding of the couple into a community of love, a community which demands fruitfulness for its own authenticity. That is what is the unique characteristic of conjugal love. And it is here that one finds the inseparable link between the unitive and procreative meaning of sexuality.

That brings about a second subtle shift in emphasis. This shift is to be found in the suggestion that love and procreation "constitute an almost indivisible unity."[13] The *almost* indivisible unity is not stressed in the commission's report, but there is the recognition that what is given in nature is not the inevitable and continuous unity of sexual love and procreation. While authentic conjugal love may well long for life-giving fruitfulness, nature has not so arranged things that love will inevitably realize that longing in the birth of children. The failure to realize fecundity is not necessarily a sign that conjugal love is inauthentic or immoral. Nor has the Church ever taught that it was. While physical impotence is an impediment to marriage in the Roman Catholic Church, known sterility is not. Conjugal love does not necessarily require fecundity in the physical sense to be authentic, as Vatican II plainly taught.[14] That recognition is fraught with significant implications.

2. Responsible Parenthood

Still in keeping with the received tradition, the commission's report insisted that "responsible parenthood ... is a fundamental requirement of a married couple's true mission."[15] Once again we encounter a claim that is beyond dispute. For who could argue that irresponsible parenthood is a good and moral thing to practice? The critical factor, however, is what one understands the content of responsible parenthood to be. Still employing general terms the commission suggested that responsible means generous and prudent,[16] before God, one another, their family and society. But what will count concretely as being generous and prudent changes with changed and changing circumstances. To determine concrete generosity and prudence is the specific decision that the consciences of the couple are forced to confront if they are to be responsible parents. Again, Vatican II clearly taught that this specific decision was to be left to the consciences of the couple.[17]

But because the commission had placed the love of the married couple at the center of its reflections, the couple's responsibility before God also appeared in a different light. The couple's vocation in marriage was to build "a stable community between man and woman, shaped by conjugal love,"[18] for this is judged to be the true basis for the procreation and education of children. The primary responsibility of any married couple before God is to develop their unity and intimacy in all its dimensions. This responsibility will at times entail the regulation of conception. "If they are to observe and cultivate all the essential values of marriage, married people need decent and human means for the regulation of conception."[19] This is essential to their vocation and their most fundamental responsibility.

It was in such a context that the commission made its revolutionary proposal, a proposal that was later explicitly rejected by Pope

Paul VI in *Humanae Vitae*,[20] and that also later was realized to have implications far beyond the one issue of birth control. The proposal went like this:

> The morality of sexual acts between married people takes its meaning first of all and specifically from the ordering of their responsible, generous and prudent parenthood. It does not then depend upon the direct fecundity of each and every particular act. Moreover the morality of every marital act depends upon the requirements of mutual love in all its aspects.[21]

The will of God for the married couple is not to be found by honoring without human interference what is given in nature. The moral law is not, the commission suggested, identical with resignation to the biological laws and processes of human life. Rather God's will is found by using what is known to be given in nature for the faithful carrying out of one's vocation—in their case, generous and prudent parenthood.[22]

Before indicating how the commission saw its proposal to be in continuity with the tradition and called for by contemporary conditions, it will be worthwhile to highlight the major changes that result from this understanding of the morality of sexual acts. In the first place, and perhaps most importantly, God's law and the laws of nature are no longer identified. More accurately, since God remains the author of the laws of nature, the moral law and the physical, chemical, biological laws of nature are not identical. Biology, chemistry, physics and all the other sciences do not provide human beings with the knowledge of laws which they are morally obliged to observe. What the sciences do provide human beings with is the knowledge of certain processes and regularities in the material world, on the basis of which they must develop moral laws which guide them in the realization of their vocation as human persons in society.

This basic change in the understanding of the natural moral law and how it is known is one of the primary grounds for the continuing dissent to *Humanae Vitae* and the charges of physicalism and biologism repeatedly made against the encyclical as well as the more recent "Declaration on Sexual Ethics." Father Charles Curran's critique of the Declaration may serve as one representative example[23] of such charges. After pointing out that the methodology adopted in the Declaration is basically the same as that used in *Humanae Vitae,*[24] Curran asserts:

> The Declaration is guilty of physicalism, since it understands sexuality primarily, if not exclusively, in the light of the physical structure of the act itself. Such a defect is clearly associated with the emphasis on the act alone and not on the person. The personal dimension of sexuality, the whole psychological aspect of human sexuality, and human sexual maturity as a goal toward which one strives are all missing. By focusing the ethical analysis unilaterally on the physical act and the faculty, there is little or no room for considerations of the psychological, the personal, the relational, the transcendent and other important aspects of human sexuality.[25]

Or, as Andrew Greeley expressed the matter in somewhat blunter and more picturesque terms, "Sex is between persons and not between organs. It is embarrassing to observe that Carl Rogers certainly perceives that and Paul VI apparently does not."[26]

The significance of this change for sexual morality may not be readily apparent to those who do not specialize in ethical theory. But to change one's basic moral norm from the givenness of physical and biological nature to the nature of the human person and his or her acts is to introduce a degree of relativity and plurality into morality where previously absoluteness and uniformity reigned. As John Giles Milhaven quickly noted, "To be able to discern the general purpose God has for the realities he created does not mean we can discern a fixed, specific purpose he has for a particular kind of act, a precise purpose which must be respected every time the act is performed."[27] From this insight he drew the appropriate conclusion: "Christians who live according to the new morality do not . . . base their moral judgments on any absolute, specific prohibitions laid down by God."[28] The functions and processes of physical nature are generally uniform and regular. But human persons are unique, historical, social and relational beings. Hence it begins to appear impossible to say *a priori* that they should always or never do this or that particular act. If this can be said about contraceptive intercourse, it can and will be said about every sexual act.

A second change to be highlighted is the suggestion that the morality of sexual acts is not to be judged in the individual, isolated case, but needs to be assessed in the context of relationships. In the particular case in point, the commission argued that the Church had indeed been right to condemn the contraceptive "way of married life which in its totality is egoistically and irrationally opposed to fruitfulness."[29] But the morality of any one act of contraceptive sexual intercourse cannot be judged apart from the total marital relationship. In practice, of course, that meant that a married couple might well decide to limit their parental fecundity to two or three children, practice contraceptive intercourse for a number of years as one means to realizing responsible parenthood, and not be judged as engaging in a contraceptive way of married life. What would be crucial to the morality of such a practice would not be the action itself, so much as the intentions or motives of the couple and the circumstances in which they lived.

The theoretical problems this analysis posed for theologians who wished to defend the traditional view was very difficult. As Richard McCormick pointed out in his analysis of *Humanae Vitae* shortly after its publication, the intrinsic link between every act of sexual intercourse and procreation is an extremely difficult analysis to sustain. In his words, "The immediate and often stated difficulty with such a contention is that, starting with an obsolete biology, it attributes a meaning to all coitus on the basis of what happens with relative rarity."[30] Yet it was the contention on which the whole argument of the papal encyclical rested, despite the challenge to it on the part of the papal commission. Furthermore, the commission's own analysis, which was clearly rejected by the encyclical, was turned down "on the grounds that an act deprived of its procreative power is intrinsically evil. But this is precisely the point to be shown. In my judgment the encyclical does not succeed in doing this."[31]

The implications of this proposed change on how the morality of the sexual act is to be judged were perceived slowly, but they follow logically enough. For if the morality of sexual acts in marriage is to be evaluated in the context of the total marital relationship and not simply in their orientation to procreation, why is not this also true of all sexual acts, including those between non-married heterosexuals and between homosexuals? Why isn't all sexual morality contextual, to be evaluated on the basis of how it enhances or debilitates human relationships? This approach to sexual morality had been employed by a number of Protestant theologians, exemplified very well by Richard F. Hettlinger's popular work, *Living with Sex: The Student's Dilemma.*[32] While generally supporting the importance of personal commitment to one's sexual partner and the relation of sexuality to procreation, he is reluctant to conclude, for example, that pre-marital intercourse is always wrong. The more contextualist the approach to morality, the less willing is the ethician to conclude to absolute prohibitions. Is the final implication of the proposed change that any sexual act may be morally right, depending only on the intentions and circumstances of the people involved?[33]

3. Change and the Tradition

It may seem odd to those not steeped in the Catholic tradition to suggest that an obvious change in moral teaching does not, as the commission put it, "contradict the genuine sense of this tradition and the purpose of the previous doctrinal condemnations...."[34] There are many reasons, practical, pastoral and theological, for seeing the change as a "further step in the doctrinal evolution" and for arguing that the "doctrine on marriage and its essential values remains the same and whole, but it is now applied differently out of a deeper understanding."[35] Those reasons, however, will be passed over here since they do not bear directly on sexual morality. But some of the commission's arguments do have immediate relevance to what is being said about sexual morality, and it is these we need to consider.

In the first place there are the changed social conditions under which contemporary human beings must live out their sexuality. Among such conditions the commission noted the following: new difficulties and new possibilities for the education of children; changes in the role of women in society and so in matrimonial and familial roles; a decrease in the rate of infant mortality; new knowledge in biology, psychology, sexuality and demography; a changed estimation of the meaning and value of human sexuality and mar-

riage; an increased sense of human responsibility for the course of
history and society; the increasingly articulate experience of the laity.
In the light of these changing conditions, the commission argued,
there develops, or should develop, "a better, deeper and more correct
understanding of conjugal life and of the conjugal act. . . ."[36]

The most obvious and explicit impact these changes have had
on sexual moral teaching was the acceptance of the moral legitimacy
of natural means of birth control. That acceptance, as the commission pointed out, "makes a separation between the sexual act which
is explicitly intended and its reproductive effect which is intentionally excluded."[37] That separation seemed to many to be very significant, yet it was difficult to explain its precise significance and its
implications. For it leads us once again into the difficult morass of
ethical theory and analysis. It may, however, be possible to present
the problem simply, if not the solution.

Morally, almost everyone is aware of the importance of good intentions. To do good a person must want to do good or at the very
least not intend to do evil. If the human person's intention or motivation in acting is morally bad, e.g., a person who takes nude photo-
graphs of his acquaintances with the precise purpose of using the
pictures for blackmail, then the action that proceeds from that intention is also morally wrong. Bad moral intentions make for immoral
acts. However, it is important to notice that, given the bad intention,
the action itself is really immaterial to the judgment of its immorality. To intend evil is what is morally wrong, whether or not it is
wrong to take nude pictures.

The story is not quite the same in regard to good intentions.
Morally it is not enough simply to mean well though it is certainly
necessary. The human person must also intend a real good that is in
proper relation to other goods that are associated with the action. A
simple example will illustrate the meaning of this requirement. A
student wants to do well on his final examination, a praiseworthy intention. He decides to realize this intention by stealing the exam
from his professor's office. Then he comes to himself and recognizes
that that choice of means makes him intent on evil rather than the
good. So he decides to achieve his purpose by studying hard. In the
course of studying, his roommate appears with a desperate plea for
help. He has had a heart attack and needs immediate medical atten-

tion. But the student, more intent on studying hard and getting a good grade (real goods), ignores his roommate's plea, preferring the good grade to his roommate's life and health. The real good he is intent on is not in proper relationship to the real goods associated with his action.

When applied to sexual morality, what is it that the married couple must intend? If procreation were the sole good of sexual intercourse, then the only morally upright intention in having sexual intercourse would be to have children. And it would be vividly clear why contraceptive intercourse was always wrong. But there is another basic good of sexual intercourse: it is an expression of and deepening of mutual love. The couple may quite legitimately intend the sexual act for this purpose. Now in doing this, in intending the sexual act as an expression of love, may they ever explicitly exclude the procreative intentionality? This is a particularly important question for a tradition which sees an inseparable link between the two goods.

It was the claim of the birth control commission that in approving of the rhythm method of birth control and other forms of natural family planning, the Church had already taught that it was permissible to intend explicitly the unitive purpose of sex and to exclude intentionally the procreative purpose. To allow artificial means as well as natural means of birth control does not change this teaching. It merely develops it to a logical conclusion. Furthermore, it means that the justification of sexual activity can occur outside a procreative setting or possibility. So those actions that were judged to be immoral because they lacked a procreative orientation, actions like masturbation, homosexual acts, bestiality, petting to orgasm and so on, have to be evaluated in different terms and in other ways.

Paul VI, of course, rejected this understanding of the Church's teaching about natural methods of birth control without any extensive attempt to show why it was wrong. In *Humanae Vitae* he did provide one clue to his reasoning. As he explained the matter, "To make use of the gift of conjugal love while respecting the laws of the generative process means to acknowledge oneself not to be the arbiter of the sources of human life, but rather the minister of the design established by the Creator."[38] That seems to suggest a transcendent referent to the intentionality proper to sexual intercourse. To turn

away from the procreative meaning by deliberate human intervention is to prefer one's own plans and purposes to God's. If this is in
fact the case, then in using artificial methods of birth control, people
are intent on a real good that is not in proper relationship to the other real goods associated with the action. However, that this is so is
declared but not established in the papal encyclical.

4. Objective Criteria of Morality

One of the more persistent features of Catholic moral teaching
has been its insistence that morality has an objectivity to it and so
moral judgments must be made according to objective norms.[39]
Again and again one reads warnings and admonitions that moral decisions are "not to be left to purely arbitrary decision."[40] Morality is
not a matter of taste or whim; it is a matter of doing the truth in love,
as the First Epistle of John expressed it.[41] Consequently, while the
individual conscience is the ultimate subjective norm of right and
wrong, the Church must concern itself with the proper formation of
conscience and so with objective norms of morality.

For most people objective criteria of morality take the form of
moral rules which they are taught and exhorted to obey. For religious people these moral rules are given divine sanction and are often
regarded as the law of God. The Ten Commandments in the Old
Testament are a good example of this process.[42] One significance that
can be attached to the Commandments is that they represent or express God's will for his people. Since it is God's authority that lies
behind the commandments, they are not to be argued with but simply obeyed. In such an understanding the very essence of morality is
obedience to God's will, and the critical question is how God makes
his will known to human beings.

In the Catholic community a complex answer was given to the
critical question. God makes his will known to human beings in various ways. He reveals it to them in the very works of creation he has
made, which for their part they come to know through the use of
reason. Understanding who and what they are by nature, they discover the natural moral law. The Church, in its official teaching office, is held to be the guardian and authentic interpreter of the
natural moral law. While aided by divine grace in fulfilling this func-

tion, the interpretation is still a work of reason which requires study and research and which is then presented as being reasonable and accessible to all humans.[43]

God also makes his will known through his activity in history, especially in the history of Israel and the life, death and resurrection of Jesus. This revelation is now mediated to human beings in the Bible. Here again the Church is charged with the preservation and transmission of the revelation. Yet it is generally agreed upon in the Catholic tradition that there are no new specific moral obligations or rules contained in the Scriptures that are not present also in the natural moral law. What would be distinctive about Christian morality would not be its specific content or moral rules, but the motivation and the transcendental intentionality of the Christian, as Joseph Fuchs among others has argued.[44] The fully human is what is truly Christian.

Finally God also makes his will known to human beings in the depths of their hearts or consciences through the enlightenment of the Holy Spirit. It is here where objective criteria are most difficult to come by, for the Spirit blows where he will and the leadings of the Spirit can only be discerned and tested; they cannot be reduced to a set of rules or objective norms. Nonetheless it is the one same God who is making his will known in nature, in Scripture, in the tradition of the Church and in the heart of human persons. So there will be no contradiction among the various sources if they are read correctly.

Given this understanding of the significance of objective criteria, what are the objective criteria for sexual morality? When expressed in general terms, there is no great dispute. The birth control commission, following Vatican II, proposed that "among these criteria, this must be put first: the action must correspond to the nature of the person and of his acts. . . ."[45] More directly pertinent to sexual morality, one can find such criteria as the nature of conjugal love,[46] the nature or structure of the conjugal act,[47] and the finality of the sexual act.[48] Only as secondary criteria do we find such things as regard for health, psychic well-being, respect for personal dignity and so forth.[49] Even so such general criteria scarcely admit of serious exception.

It is the method of spelling out these criteria that gives rise to the dispute. The tendency of the official teaching has been to articulate the criteria in terms of laws so that the primary obligation of the person is to respect the law of God, whether one agrees with or understands the reason for the law in the first place. And since the Church is the authentic interpreter of the natural moral law, is aided in this task by divine grace, and the authority of its teaching is not dependent on the excellence of its reasons and arguments,[50] sexual morality involves conforming one's behavior to the laws and teaching of the Church. It is not necessary for the official teaching office to explain how it knows that these are, indeed, God's laws. Nor is it the task of the theologian to dispute the teaching. Rather the theological task is to find reasons supporting the teaching.

A second way of articulating the criteria governing sexuality is in terms of consequences. If sexuality is ordered to marriage and family, any action which promotes the well-being of the marriage and the family, or which helps ready persons for marriage and family, would be regarded as morally good. Intimations of this approach can be found in the commission's insistence on objective criteria as being "the conditions for keeping and fostering the essential values of marriage as a community of fruitful love."[51] In such a model the transcendent referent of Christian morality is present, but less evident. The person responds to God not directly in every act of obedience, but in carrying out his or her calling to create a community of fruitful love.

A third way of developing the criteria guiding sexual morality is to develop more personalistic and relational terms and then to articulate the general criteria with the individual persons as the central focus, rather than the institutions of marriage and family or the laws of God and nature. In this model the transcendent referent of Christian morality is much less clear. It is the growth and well-being of human persons that appears to be the central concern. The human person responds to God by and in responding in love to his or her neighbors. To put the matter in a different way, this model suggests that we discover God's law not in an analysis of nature, though surely such analysis has a place, nor in some ideal image of what one's vocation demands, though ideals provide direction and intelligibility for our actions, but in the living, changing needs and possibilities of one's neighbor.

The experience of Joseph Fletcher's *Situation Ethics* had made it clear that an ethic based on love could not succeed without norms, without objective criteria for action. As Herbert McCabe had pointed out in his insightful book, *What Is Ethics All About?*: "We cannot be sure beforehand what might turn out to be loving behavior, but if we can't say of any behavior at all that it is definitely *not* loving behavior, then I think the word 'love' would be hopelessly vague. I mean that if a word is to be meaningful there must be at least something that it doesn't mean, however open-ended it may otherwise be."[52]

In its essential form, therefore, the discussion about sexual morality hinges very much on the question of ethical epistemology, on how anyone knows that a particular act is sometimes, always or never good, that a particular duty or obligation is, in fact, a law of God and so to be done.

Three studies, in particular, have appeared in recent years seeking to clarify this question in regard to sexual morality in general and specific sexual practices in particular. Therefore they will occupy the major part of our attention in the next two chapters.

Notes

1. Noonan, *Contraception,* pp. 438–447; on pp. 450–475 there is a thorough discussion of the debate.

2. "Address of Pope Paul VI to a General Audience, July 31, 1968," Liebard, 1230, p. 349.

3. Forty-one of the fifty members endorsed the change. That percentage seems to reflect closely current American Catholic opinion on the morality of contraception. See *National Catholic Reporter,* April 19, 1967.

4. Charles E. Curran, Robert E. Hunt *et al., Dissent in and for the Church.*

5. Joseph J. Farraher, S.J., "Contraception" (this reference is contained in my personal notes; I have as yet been unable to track it down).

6. "The Theological Report of the Papal Commission on Birth

Control, June 26, 1966"; "Papal Commission on Birth Control: Pastoral Approaches, June 26, 1966"; Liebard, pp. 296–320.

7. *Ibid.,* 1047–1051, pp. 298–299.

8. A representative sampling of Protestant authors: Paul Ramsey, "A Christian Approach to the Question of Sexual Relations Outside of Marriage," *The Journal of Religion* 45 (1965), pp. 100–118; Richard F. Hettlinger, *Living With Sex: The Student's Dilemma* (New York: Seabury Press, 1966); Peter Bertocci, *Sex, Love and the Person* (Kansas City: Sheed Andrews and McMeel, Inc., 1967).

9. A point frequently made by Charles E. Curran, "Sin and Sexuality," *Themes in Fundamental Moral Theology* (Notre Dame: University Press, 1977), pp. 180–184.

10. "Papal Commission," Liebard, 1050, p. 299.

11. *Ibid.,* 1066, p. 304.

12. Curran, "Sin and Sexuality," pp. 178–179.

13. See note 10.

14. *Gaudium et Spes,* 50.

15. "Papal Commission," Liebard, 1053, p. 300.

16. *Ibid.*

17. *Gaudium et Spes,* 50.

18. "Papal Commission," Liebard, 1055, p. 300.

19. *Ibid.,* 1060, p. 302.

20. *Humanae Vitae,* Liebard, 1194, p. 338.

21. "Papal Commission," Liebard, 1063, pp. 302–303.

22. *Ibid.,* 1061, p. 302.

23. The charge is very common. It has been rebutted by, among others, Joseph J. Farraher, S.J., "Contraception," *New Catholic Encyclopedia,* XVI, Supplement 1967–1974 (New York: McGraw-Hill, 1974), p. 103.

24. Charles E. Curran, "Sexual Ethics: A Critique," *Issues in Sexual and Medical Ethics* (Notre Dame: University of Notre Dame Press, 1978), p. 38.

25. *Ibid.,* p. 40.

26. Andrew M. Greeley, *The New Agenda* (Garden City: Doubleday & Co., 1973), pp. 142–143.

27. John Giles Milhaven, *Toward A New Catholic Morality* (Garden City: Doubleday & Co., Inc., 1970), p. 60.

28. *Ibid.,* p. 61.

29. "Papal Commission," Liebard, 1064, p. 303.

30. Richard A. McCormick, *Notes on Moral Theology 1965 Through 1980* (Washington, D.C.: University Press of America, 1980), January–June 1968, p. 218.

31. *Ibid.,* pp. 220–221.

32. Cf. note 8.

33. Curran, "Sin and Sexuality," p. 189, n. 39.

34. "Papal Commission," Liebard, 1067, p. 304.

35. *Ibid.,* 1069, p. 304.

36. *Ibid.*

37. *Ibid.,* 1070, p. 305.

38. *Humanae Vitae,* Liebard, 1191, p. 337.

39. A great deal of work has been done in recent years on the question of moral norms. Among the most important works are Charles E. Curran and Richard A. McCormick (eds.), *Readings in Moral Theology No. 1: Moral Norms and Catholic Tradition* (Ramsey: Paulist Press, 1979); Richard A. McCormick and Paul Ramsey (eds.), *Doing Evil To Achieve Good* (Chicago: Loyola University Press, 1978); John R. Connery, S.J., "Catholic Ethics: Has the Norm for Rule-Making Changed?" *Theological Studies* 42 (June 1981), pp. 232–250; Norbert J. Rigali, S.J., "Evil and Models of Christian Ethics," *Horizons* 8 (Spring 1981), pp. 7–22.

40. For example, "Papal Commission," Liebard, 1074, p. 306.

41. 1 Jn 3:18–19.

42. Burtchaell, pp. 53–58.

43. Paul VI reviewed these claims in *Humanae Vitae,* Liebard, 1168, pp. 332–333; 1190, pp. 336–337.

44. Joseph Fuchs, S.J., *Human Values and Christian Morality* (London: Gill and Macmillan, 1970), pp. 120–134. A more complete discussion of the issue can be found in Charles E. Curran and Richard A. McCormick (eds.), *Readings in Moral Theology No. 2: The Distinctiveness of Christian Ethics* (Ramsey: Paulist Press, 1980).

45. "Papal Commission," Liebard, 1081, p. 307.

46. *Humanae Vitae,* Liebard, 1175, p. 334.

47. *Ibid.,* 1190, p. 336.

48. "Declaration," Liebard, 1536, p. 437.

49. "Papal Commission: Pastoral Approaches," Liebard, 1120, p. 318.

50. McCormick, *Notes on Moral Theology 1965 Through 1980,* pp. 261–266.

51. "Papal Commission," Liebard, 1080, p. 307.

52. McCabe, p. 20.

4
Revised Approaches
to Sexual Morality

The widespread, but by no means universal, discontent with the official Church teaching on sexual morality had a twofold focus. The disagreement was both methodological and substantive. For the ordinary Catholic the important disagreement was substantive; he or she simply did not agree that all methods of artificial contraception were seriously disordered acts, or that pre-marital sex was always wrong, or that a second marriage after divorce was never permissible.[1] For most theologians, however, the methodological disagreement was primary. Writing in response to the Vatican "Declaration on Sexual Ethics," Charles Curran argued that "the methodological approach of the Catholic tradition as incorporated in this document and *Humanae Vitae* needs to be criticized and changed."[2] Andrew Greeley insisted that his "argument at this point is not so much with the conclusion of *Humanae Vitae* (though I don't accept that either) but with the resolute refusal to see that in different contexts different approaches are necessary."[3] Many other theologians were voicing the same claim in one way or another.[4] They were looking for a new way to think about sexuality and morality.

There also existed a slowly developing consensus on what the revised approach should look like. A pastoral letter by the bishop of Brooklyn, New York, Francis Mugavero, on sexuality won wide acclaim for its positive, compassionate and supportive tone, as well as its direct language.[5] Richard McCormick, in his comments on the letter, pointed out the significance of the tone and language.

> Mugavero's language and tone meet people where they are. Tone, in moral matters, is not everything, but it is enormously important; for it reveals attitudes toward persons, norms, conflicts, God, the human condition. Because this is so, tone not only affects communicability; at some point it also cuts close to the basic value judgments themselves. . . . That is why a document that is tonally inadequate risks being substantially incomplete or even wrong.[6]

Greeley had made somewhat the same point in arguing for the recognition of changed conditions. "In a sense," he wrote, "sexuality has been turned upside down. It is now thought to be virtuous not to have more children but fewer. Sexual intercourse is not an obligation but a fulfillment. Sexual desires are not bad, they are good. Sex does not imprison man, it liberates him."[7] It seemed clear to Greeley that any "sexual teaching that does not address itself to this changed situation, however wise it may be, simply will have no impact at all."[8]

The desire for a new approach to sexuality and morality had, perhaps, its most dramatic expression at the 1980 Synod of Bishops in Rome. Both the presentation of Archbishop Joseph L. Bernardin of Cincinnati and the intervention of Archbishop John R. Quinn of San Francisco drew wide attention in their call for a more positive approach to sexuality.[9] Father Richard McBrien called Bernardin's presentation one of the most substantive delivered at the Synod and expressed his own similar conviction.

> What the Catholic Church needs is not more hand-wringing over non-compliance, but a positive doctrine of sexuality that can gain the respect of those to whom it is directed: a doctrine that recognizes the intrinsic goodness of sexuality and that acknowledges the radical equality of the human race, male and female alike.[10]

But as the bishops' discussions at the Synod indicated and as McBrien also pointed out, "the problem is not only one of communication, although it is clearly that. The problem is also one of substance and comment."[11] What would a new, more positive approach mean for substantive teaching on divorce and remarriage, homosexual acts, pre-marital relations, and so on?

In the midst of the search for a new way of thinking about sexuality, several books, sympathetic to a revised approach, have appeared which provide us with some indication of how sexual morality will be affected. The committee study, *Human Sexuality,* sponsored by The Catholic Theological Society of America (CTSA),[12] is one such work. The Canadian scholar, Andre Guindon, produced a second such book, *The Sexual Language.*[13] Philip Keane's *Sexual Morality: A Catholic Perspective* is a third. These three works have the advantage of presenting the reader with a reasonably systematic and extensive view of sexual morality which touches on many substantive questions rather than focusing exclusively on one or two. In them the interplay between method and substance can be clearly seen. Accordingly this chapter will examine at length the ground-breaking study of the CTSA in terms of both its methodology and substantive conclusions, and some of the critical response to it. The next chapter will consider the alternative methods proposed by Keane and Guindon, and the critique of such revised proposals by Germain Grisez, William May and others.

Human Sexuality—Methodology

1. General Approach

Of the three books, the CTSA committee study has been the most controversial and has come in for the most criticism.[14] The authors consciously adopted an approach to sexual morality that is historical, personalist and relational, and appealed especially to Vatican II in defense of this choice.[15] Simply explained these three words are an effort to state an understanding of what it is to be a human being. As historical, the human being, in his or her thinking, valuing and acting, is culturally limited and constantly in the process of change. Human nature is not a complete, fixed, static reality, but an unfinished, dynamic, changing reality. Human being is about growth and development, the ultimate horizons of which are always beyond us. In practice that means that Christian ideals and values will need an ever changing application as sociological, historical and cultural conditions change, along with the Christian self-understanding of those ideals and values.

The personalist approach involves a double recognition. First, as Greeley had suggested in another context, it is a recognition that "one should consider not the attributes of the [marital] union between persons but rather the persons themselves."[16] It is the human person who is central to ethical consideration, and it is personal human dignity that morality is intended to serve. Interestingly enough this approach has been much more in evidence in the Church's teachings on social justice than in its teachings on sexual morality.[17] To paraphrase a scriptural saying about the sabbath, marriage exists for human beings; human beings do not exist for marriage. The second recognition involved in the personalist approach is that acts are abstractions. There is no such thing in reality as an act in itself. There are only acting persons. Consequently the moral quality of any action cannot be evaluated apart from the subjective intentions of the acting subjects.

Finally to adopt a relational approach to morality is to acknowledge the human person as a social being. To be a human person is to be in relation to other persons, to be interpersonal. Human acting is acting in a social world. Action either establishes and strengthens bonds between the agent and other persons in the world or it destroys or weakens those bonds. Nor is moral behavior a "simple matter between man and men; [it is also] creative of bonds with the Lord."[18] Once again, therefore, actions cannot be evaluated apart from their relational context and they must be evaluated in terms of their relational significance. The authors of *Human Sexuality* express all this clearly:

> It is not surprising then that recent developments in moral theology have called into serious doubt the impersonalism, legalism, and minimalism that often result from such an act-oriented approach. Focusing on the isolated act and assigning it an inviolable moral value in the abstract left little room for consideration of the personal and interpersonal

values that are central to genuine morality. Modern trends, returning to some of the emphases observed in Sacred Scripture, in the Middle Ages, and in the theology of St. Thomas, prefer to give greater importance to attitude over act, to pattern or habit over the isolated instance, and to the intersubjective and social over the abstract and individual.[19]

2. Sexuality

With this understanding of the human to guide the discussion, the next task is to delineate what it means to be a sexual person. How is human sexuality to be defined? It is important to grasp the significance of the question as well as the answer. For sexuality can be, and has been, understood as a drive or an appetite, on a par with the appetites we call hunger and thirst. It becomes something that happens to us. We get hungry, we get thirsty, we get sexually aroused. On this model sexuality is an event, albeit a recurring event, of our experience.

Defining sexuality in this way can lead in one of two directions. Just as the appetites of hunger and thirst have their natural satisfaction in food and drink, so does the sexual appetite have its natural satisfaction in orgasm. In the same way that the human person needs the satisfaction of food and drink, so, too, he or she needs sexual satisfaction and has as much right to it as to food and drink. This is clearly the understanding of sexuality that underlies a popular sex manual like David Reuben's *Everything You Always Wanted To Know About Sex,*[20] as well as the popular Christian situation ethics of the Roys[21] mentioned earlier. Reuben is quite explicit: "Sex is one of the few renewable pleasures in this life. It is tragic for man to allow his emotions to deprive him of what is justly his. . . ."[22] In this view it is not necessary to deny that other values than fun are related to sex, but they are neither necessary nor intrinsically related to one another. To quote Reuben again:

> The ideal act of sexual intercourse combines reproduction, deep mutual love, and profound physical pleasure. Most people will experience this combination less than a dozen

times in their life span. If they are very fortunate, they will frequently be able to combine an expression of love with a real physical enjoyment of sex. But at the very minimum intercourse should provide the maximum sexual gratification possible to both man and woman. If they can accomplish that, at least it is a first step toward achieving the rest.[23]

But understanding human sexuality as one drive or appetite among others does not always lead to such a hedonistic permissiveness. For it is clear that human beings do not need sexual satisfaction with quite the same necessity as they need food and drink. Indeed it is not human individuals who need sex but the human species which needs it for survival. The right to sexual gratification, therefore, is entailed or warranted not by a personal need but by a social need— the need for procreation. So understanding sexuality as one human appetite among others leads to a position which finds sexual expression justified either by pleasure or by procreation.

Such a definition of sexuality is rejected by the authors of *Human Sexuality* as being too narrow and incompatible with human experience and with contemporary scientific understanding: "Sex is seen as a force that permeates, influences, and affects every act of a person's being at every moment of existence. It is not operative in one restricted area of life but is rather at the core and center of our total life-response."[24] "Sexuality, therefore, needs to be understood not as an action but as the way of being in, and relating to, the world as a *male* or *female* person."[25] Sexuality is not something we have and show off to others in action, like a musical skill. Sexuality is what we are, and sexual expression is, therefore, always and inevitably self-expression. To quote the study again, "sexuality then is the mode or manner by which humans experience and express both the incompleteness of their individualities as well as their relatedness to each other as male or female."[26]

3. Basic Norm

The implications of this definition of sexuality deserve some explanation. First, sexuality is neither morally good nor morally bad. It

just is, and as created and intended by God, it shares in the basic ontic goodness of all creation. Second, sexuality carries with it a task,
or, in more religious terms, a mission, as does the gift of life itself.
Every man is called to become fully man; every woman is called to
become fully woman. Sexuality is at one and the same time the basis
for human growth to full personal maturity and also a means to that
growth. For full growth into manhood and womanhood, man and
woman must relate to each other. They have the need for one another in order "to experience the fullness of being-with-another in
the human project" and "to realize the potential for sharing subjec-
tivity."[27] Third, sexuality is bodily and impels and attracts one bodily
existence to another. Our sexuality moves us to pay attention to others, to look, to reach out and touch and feel others, to enter upon
what Peter Bertocci has called the sexual progression which moves
us toward the search for greater, physical intimacy.[28] As the authors
of the CTSA study express it, sexuality calls "people to a clearer recognition of their relational nature, of their absolute need to reach out
and embrace others to achieve personal fulfillment. Sexuality is the
Creator's ingenious way of calling people out of themselves into relationship with others."[29]

   Based on this understanding of sexuality, what is the appropriate norm to express the purpose of sexuality? Can the traditional
double meaning of sexuality as unitive and procreative express this
understanding or is another norm required? Finding limitations in
the traditional norm, the basic proposal made in *Human Sexuality* is
that the expression "creative growth toward integration"[30] more ade-
quately states the basic normative purpose of sexuality. That sexual
behavior is morally right or in accord with God's will which contrib-
utes to the creative growth toward integration of human persons in
relationship. At the same time it is clear that such a norm is still inadequate for the moral evaluation of specific actions and that additional criteria are required. That leads the authors to a second
important proposal.

4. Other Norms

   The authors are reluctant to ask the traditional question "Is this
act morally right or wrong?" even while recognizing that it is hu-

manly inevitable. Therefore, in keeping with their more positive approach, they suggest the possibility of developing additional norms for sexual behavior by articulating "some of the values which sexuality ought to preserve and promote...."[31] Instead of pointing out what is wrong with sex, perhaps it is possible to point out what is right or good about it and use such values as criteria for judging individual acts. This proposal is worth dwelling on briefly.

Most moral norms that take the form of rules or laws, and which are addressed to human actions rather than attitudes, are expressed in negatives—thou shalt not. That is not surprising since it is vastly easier to decide and say that something is morally wrong than to decide and say that it is morally right. Its moral rightness always depends on the subjective intentions of the agent, the circumstances in which the action is placed and the consequences of the act. In general terms it is good to be kind to one's neighbor but what counts specifically as a kind act is not so clear. Lending one's neighbor a hundred dollars may or may not be the kind thing to do. Where the purpose of sexuality is defined in such personal, psychological terms as creative growth toward integration, and one wishes to sustain the positive mode of discourse, it is simply not possible to express the goods that sexuality serves in terms of concrete, specific actions. The norms will not enable anyone to arrive at universal moral absolutes. They are, therefore, proposed as guidelines, not rules, which leave to the individual conscience a larger sphere of responsibility.

As a final step, then, before considering specific modes of sexual conduct, the authors present seven values which morally appropriate sexual behavior should serve. It is their contention that when "such qualities prevail, one can be reasonably sure that the sexual behavior that has brought them forth is wholesome and moral."[32] The seven values singled out as particularly significant are self-liberating, other-enriching, honest, faithful, socially responsible, life-serving and joyous.[33] A brief word of explanation on each of these seven values is in order.

Self-liberating does not catch exactly what the authors had in mind in insisting on this value, as their own explanation makes clear. What they want acknowledged is the "legitimate self-interest and self-fulfillment that sexual expression is meant to serve and satisfy."[34]

It is unrealistic and harmful to speak of a sexual relationship as a selfless giving of oneself to the other. There is something to be received as well as to be given, so that sexual behavior which is done merely as a duty or because one's partner enjoys it or demands it is perceived to be a form of self-enslavement. The second value of other-enriching is but the other side of the coin. There should be something in sexual behavior for one's partner as well as for oneself. It is not sufficient, according to the authors, that the sexual behavior is non-coercive and non-manipulative of one's partner. It must make a positive contribution to the growth toward personal wholeness of one's partner. These two values, therefore, seem to be an alternate way of insisting that sexual behavior should be genuinely an expression of love and concern for the other and an enhancement of, a deepening of, that love. Sexual activity should express love and make love in the very expression.

The value of honesty as associated with sexual conduct speaks mainly to a correspondence between the form of sexual expression and the depth of the personal relationship that exists between the two partners. Sexual expression, precisely as a form of personal expression, demands truthfulness for its moral integrity. It should be an expression of what one authentically feels and wishes to say. The authors warn of the difficulty in sustaining an honest sexual relationship, but they do not advert to the fact that the next three values are intrinsically related to the demand for honesty.

Faithfulness or fidelity is the study's bow to the more traditional insistence on monogamy and indissolubility in marriage. Because they are working with a wider meaning of sexuality than simply genital behavior, and a wider set of relationships than simply marriage, marital fidelity is but one instance of fidelity. "In marriage, this fidelity is called to a perfection unmatched at any other level and establishing a very special, distinct, and particular relationship."[35] Unfortunately, because of this wider context, it becomes next to impossible to say what fidelity means in specifically sexual behavior. The virtue of fidelity protects and promotes stable relationships, the authors rightly assert. But they do not explain what fidelity means.

The value of socially responsible sexuality attacks the mistaken notion that sex is a private matter and that it is no one's business what anyone else does sexually. Whatever minor merit that idea may have as a legal directive, it is morally false. Sexual behavior and sexual relationships are fraught with significance for the common good, the well-being of the social order as a whole. Morality demands that any sexual expression contribute to the building up of the human community. Again the tradition drew the conclusion that monogamous, indissoluble marriage was an essential requirement of socially responsible sex. This study merely asserts that "the precise implications of this responsibility may vary considerably with time, place and culture. . . ."[36]

Because there is an intimate relationship between the creative and integrative aspects of sexuality, every expression of sexuality is called upon to be life-serving, not necessarily life-giving. It is the wider meaning of sexuality that accounts for the shift from life-giving to life-serving. This is useful in indicating how the celibate and single living out of one's sexuality is called to be and can be life-serving. It fails, however, to show how explicit sexual behavior as such is or can be life-serving if it is deliberately contraceptive in intent. The authors do conclude, however, that sexual intercourse "with an accompanying abortive intent should procreation ensue would be a clear contradiction of this life-serving quality of human sexuality."[37]

Finally, sexuality should be joyous. As a seventh-value criterion, it does not differ significantly from the first two norms, at least as the authors explain it. "Human sexual expression is meant to be enjoyed."[38] The one new note they add is the suggestion that sexual expression is to be understood as a celebration of life and love, a notion to which we will return in the final chapter.

These norms proposed for the objective evaluation of the morality of sexual behavior by the CTSA committee have been criticized for their psychologism, their self-oriented character and their mushy character.[39] Richard McCormick and Daniel Maguire both find them to be lacking in a sex-specific character.[40] They are values that properly belong to any relationship, not specifically to a sexual relationship. Consequently in applying these norms to specific sexual behavior, the study is not very definite or specific in giving answers. So we will turn to this application next, considering, in turn, autosexual, heterosexual and homosexual practices.

Human Sexuality—Application

1. Autosexual Acts

The term "autosexual" is designed to cover those sexual activities that one engages in alone. It is borrowed from Philip Keane,[41] and includes such things as masturbation, bestiality, fetishism, transvestism, sex-change operations, pornography and obscenity, fantasies and daydreams. Under this heading is also included what is proper to those committed to living in the single state. Since masturbation is the most common of the acts to be considered, it will be treated first.

Masturbation, understood as the deliberate manipulation of the genitals with a view to orgasm, has traditionally been understood as a seriously disordered act and an objectively grave evil, a position repeated by the "Declaration on Sexual Ethics." While the practice may at times be compulsive and so the subjective culpability of the person is lessened or even absent, this is not usually to be presumed. The CTSA study finds this position too simple. "Masturbation is a subtle and complex phenomenon. To condemn every act of masturbation harshly as mortal sin or to dismiss it lightly as of no moral consequence fails to do justice to the symptomatic nature of masturbation capable of many meanings."[42]

Accordingly the study distinguishes six types of masturbation, all of which are to be evaluated differently and which require different pastoral approaches. However, in keeping with the emphasis on attitude rather than act, two general guidelines are proposed. A single act or even occasional acts of willful masturbation are not to be judged as placing an individual in the state of mortal sin, for they do not represent a substantial or serious disordering or inversion of the sexual order. Masturbation is not the sort of action that deeply engages one's personhood and effects a substantial change in one's basic orientation to the good. Second, whatever the type of masturbation, little is achieved by focusing on the behavior itself. That only complicates the problem by driving the person deeper into himself or herself in guilt-ridden anxiety.

Among the six types of masturbation only hedonistic masturbation, that which is done "simply for the pleasure involved, without any effort at control or integration,"[43] has the possibility of being a serious moral disorder. It is agreed that such a use of one's sexuality "creates a serious obstacle to personal growth and integration." Even here it is suggested only that this may be the case, and it is hard to see any grounds for rebutting a claim like Betty Dodson's *Liberating Masturbation,*[44] which praises the liberating and creative possibilities of deliberate and pleasure-seeking masturbation for self-love and other-love.

Adolescent masturbation is perceived as a phase of life, not to be taken with great moral seriousness, while the youth is encouraged and directed to reach out to others. As he does so the phase will pass. Compensatory masturbation as an outlet for an unhappy home life, and pathological masturbation—a result of psychological maladjustment—are more in need of understanding and possibly counseling than of moral evaluation. Masturbation of necessity, as a relief from strong sexual tensions in the absence of the more normal outlet, is said "to be a matter of prudent choice of values. Moral malice in such instances ought not to be imputed."[45] Finally, masturbation for medical reasons, e.g., to obtain sperm for a fertility test, is not only not immoral in any way, but promotes the life-serving value of sexuality.

In regard to the other forms of autosexual behavior, fetishism, bestiality and transvestism are judged more as pathological behaviors in need of psychological help than as moral disorders. Sex-change operations are regarded as highly experimental procedures, which they surely are, but not to be rejected out of hand. Finally in regard to pornography and obscenity, the study sees "a goodly amount of explicitly sexual material to be neuter or amoral to most adults,"[46] but harmful when it results in the exploitation of people. The study does not discuss daydreams and fantasies and offers only a repetition of the norm of creative growth toward integration for those living in the single state.

2. Heterosexual Acts

The issues to be discussed under this heading are numerous—too many, in fact, for all of them to receive treatment here. The study, as part of its discussion of marital sexuality, considers the issues of contraception, sterilization, artificial insemination, child-free marriage, common-law marriages, so-called open marriages, swinging, adultery, and communal living. In discussing non-marital sexuality it covers pre-marital relations, dating and courtship. What the study is saying about sexual morality can be conveyed by considering its treatment of two issues, swinging and pre-marital sex.

Swinging, or free sex, is recognized as a radical departure from the value of fidelity in sexual relationships, often inspired by a desire for personal gratification or what used to be called the satisfaction of lust. Empirical studies show that such practices often prove unsatisfying and even alienating to those who take part in them. On this basis, the study concludes, "While remaining open to the results of further research, we find that ... swinging seems destructive and alienating and therefore generally dehumanizing."[47] When this somewhat tentative conclusion was criticized by Daniel Maguire as being insufficiently negative—he preferred to put swinging "in the category of *the unimaginable exception*"[48]—one author of the report defended the conclusion as admittedly "less conclusive, and more tentative but consistent with the available data."[49]

In the discussion of pre-marital sexual relations one clear guideline is given: "Dishonesty is certainly involved when a man engages in sexual intercourse with a woman with whom he would not want to have a child."[50] The study, therefore, dismisses as irresponsible both casual sexual encounters that are merely recreational and even those that are caring but not part of building a stable and lasting relationship. However, in the context of a serious and developing commitment by the partners to one another, the moral appropriateness of pre-marital sex is left to the judgment of the individuals in the light of the value criteria previously mentioned.

3. Homosexual Acts

The moral problem in regard to homosexuality is not with the existence of a homosexual orientation, but with the proper expression of that orientation, i.e., with overt homosexual acts. For in the traditional view such acts are seriously and intrinsically disordered since they lack all procreative possibility and orientation. Hence the homosexual was condemned to a life of involuntary celibacy, and all too often a life of secrecy and guilt. Not knowing the cause of homosexual orientation, how to change such orientation, or even whether such a change is possible or desirable, it is, as the study recognizes, "difficult to say anything about homosexuality that is not of a provisional nature."[51]

Three other preliminary points are to be noted. The cultural antipathy to homosexuality, the almost pathological fear of it which leads parents to disown children and friend to betray friend, makes rational discussion of the subject extremely difficult. It is almost impossible for the heterosexual to comprehend the outlook and the problems of the homosexual who is like him or her in all things except sexual orientation. The unnaturalness of homosexuality and so the immorality of homosexual acts seems almost self-evident to the heterosexual. But that, of course, has not always been the case.[52]

Despite the lack of knowledge about homosexuality, there has been a growing interest in learning more in the last forty years. As the CTSA study noted, *Homosexuality: An Annotated Bibliography* contains 1,265 entries of books and articles in the English language alone for the years 1940–1968.[53] Studies like John Boswell's, already referred to, and John McNeil's *The Church and the Homosexual*[54] have forced us to look at the biblical and historical condemnations of homosexuality in a new light. Theologians like Charles Curran and John Giles Milhaven[55] had suggested alternate approaches to the morality of homosexual acts, though no consensus of understanding emerged even among revisionists on either method or substance.

The third point to be noted is the acute theoretical and pastoral problem that homosexuality presents to Catholic sexual morality. If both theologically and pastorally Christians are to proclaim a message of good news and express loving concern for others, then homosexuality becomes almost a test case for the adequacy of one's theology and pastoral practice. Something better than "You're a sinner, so repent" has to be said. If Paul wrote to the Corinthians that it was better to marry than to burn, are homosexuals to be offered no choice but to burn?

In approaching homosexual acts, therefore, the committee faced a delicate situation. They found four basic positions being advanced about the morality of homosexual acts. The traditional position was that such acts are always objectively grave evil and intrinsically disordered. This position, based on an understanding of the human person and of sexuality which they had already rejected, and arrived at by an ethical methodology already declared inadequate, they found unconvincing.[56] At the other extreme was the position often adopted by organized homosexual groups that such acts are altogether natural and unambiguously good and require no moral limits or justification beyond not being coercive. This view they found hard to accept as ethically serious and saw it as a likely attempt at self-justification.[57]

The other two views on the morality of homosexual acts currently being proposed have significant theoretical differences, but both are open to the possibility of morally acceptable, active homosexual relationships. The first view, proposed by Curran in the articles cited, insists on the normative ideal of heterosexual relationships, affirming that human sexuality finds its fullest meaning in the relationship of love between a male and a female. In short, the ideal is for human sexuality to have both unitive and procreative meaning. But since the ideal is not always possible for everyone, "it may be necessary at times to accept, albeit reluctantly, homosexual expressions and unions as the lesser of two evils, or as the only way in which some persons can find a satisfying degree of humanity in their lives."[58] In short, stable, faithful homosexual unions would be morally permissible though never the ideal of what human sexuality ought to be.

The CTSA study-committee rejected this choice for three reasons. They challenged as unproven the claim that heterosexual behavior should always be regarded as the ideal of sexuality. Indeed, though they do not say so, it might be considered to be the very point in question. Second, if the ideal is not capable of realization because of factors that are simply unchangeable, factors of one's own selfhood, how can it be an ideal for such persons? Something else must be an ideal for them. It is this point that Maguire picks up and develops in his justification of homosexual relationships.[59] Third, this still negative view of homosexuality as less than ideal is an infringement of human dignity if heterosexuality is not the ideal. It tells people that they are living less than an ideal life through no fault of their own and reduces them, as it were, to the status of second-classs Christians.

The final current position on homosexual morality is the one that the study accepts as its own: "Homosexual acts are to be evaluated in terms of their relational significance."[60] Even so, they ask for a more detailed explanation of how the value criteria they have proposed would be met in homosexual relations, especially the demand that sexuality be life-serving for others beyond the two sexual partners.

This extensive discussion of *Human Sexuality* deserves a few comments by way of conclusion. The major problem most Catholic theologians have with the study is the tentative and uncertain judgments about the morality of actions it continually makes. There is, of course, a reason for this tentativeness. The study wants to focus on the attitudes and character of the moral agents rather than focus on acts taken in an abstract way. In doing this, however, they do not effect a closer unity between the subjective and objective poles of morality. Instead they create a wider separation. For example, if it is even imaginably possible to engage in swinging in a morally permissible way, it could only be because of changes in the moral agents themselves, not in what it is they are doing. If Christian conjugal love in all its dimensions finds its meaning in reflecting the steadfast love of Christ for his Church, and multiple sexual relationships are compatible with that meaning, then what one does and what one means by it have no discernible relationship to one another. Actions can mean whatever the agents want them to mean. If we push that to its logical, if extreme, conclusion, the death and resurrection of Jesus are salvific only because Christians choose to interpret them that way, and not in that they declared their saving quality because they found that meaning there.

A second major difficulty already referred to is that the basic norm of creative growth toward integration and the seven value criteria are not sex-specific. That is, they apply across the board to all human relationships and not specifically to sexual relationships. Again this is the result of the deliberate widening of the meaning of sexuality. While this expansion of meaning is useful in some ways, it proves deceptive in other ways. It is true, for example, that celibate sexuality, i.e., the choice of a life of committed celibacy, should not involve the rejection or suppression of one's sexuality, but should be self-liberating, other-enriching, joyous and so on. But it should also be celibate and refrain from those overt sexual expressions that make it something else. The sexual celibate[61] who finds heavy petting, passionate exchanges and possibly even sexual intercourse helpful for growth toward integration is not living sexual celibacy.

Similarly, the deliberately willed, child-free marriage will hopefully be found joyous, honest, life-serving and so on. What needs to be asked, however, is whether this way of life counts as marital sexuality. The point here is not that there are no good reasons for such a child-free marriage, but that those reasons need to do with marriage and not simply with what makes for good relationships in general. In the same way, for example, granting the various types and meanings of masturbation, Christian freedom does not see orgasmic release as necessary,[62] nor as an essential and primary means of coming to self-acceptance and self-love. Psychological defenses of masturbation ignore that it is a sexual act.

Finally, the ethical methodology of the study has been criticized, perhaps not always fairly, as being excessively psychological and consequentialist.[63] Everything seems to hinge upon the impact or consequences that an action will have upon the creative and integrated personality of the people affected by the act. Now despite the urgings of the authors for a more positive and less minimalist morality, it is hard to see how they can find moral fault with an action that does no good but also does no harm. Quickly, then, it appears that the minimal norm for sexual morality is something like the popular slogan: Anything is all right as long as nobody gets hurt. Unless there are some moral rules forbidding certain kinds of action, be they absolute prohibitions or virtually-exceptionless rules, we will not know what we mean by getting hurt. If we don't expect anything, we won't get hurt.

Therefore, other methodological proposals appear seeking better ways to analyze and understand the morality of sexual behavior in a more rigorous way. Some are partly sympathetic to the approach taken by *Human Sexuality;* others are hostile. But with the groundwork of the new approach now laid, we turn to examine them.

Notes

1. The American bishops recognized this disagreement in a statement written in preparation for the 1974 Synod of Bishops. Cf. National Conference of Catholic Bishops, *A Review of the Principal Trends in the Life of the Catholic Church in the United States* (Washington, D.C.: USCC Publications Office, 1974), p. 6: "Catholics are tolerant of abortion in at least some circumstances, reject official Church teaching on means of family limitation, have a divorce rate not markedly different from other Americans, and regard most social issues very much as their non-Catholic countrymen do."

2. Curran, "Sexual Ethics: A Critique," p. 50.

3. Greeley, *The New Agenda,* p. 139.

4. McCormick, *Notes on Moral Theology,* pp. 668–682.

5. Francis J. Mugavero, "Sexuality—God's Gift: A Pastoral Letter," *Catholic Mind* 74, No. 1303 (May 1976), pp. 53–58.

6. McCormick, pp. 679–680.

7. Greeley, p. 139.

8. *Ibid.*

9. A report on the Synod is found in Murphy, pp. 49–56.

10. Richard McBrien, "Catholics and Sexuality," *The Florida Catholic* 41 (October 31, 1980), p. 13.

11. *Ibid.*

12. It is important to note the Foreword of this book. The CTSA received the study, neither approving nor disapproving its contents. The membership was considerably divided over it.

13. Andre Guindon, *The Sexual Language* (Ottawa: The University of Ottawa Press, 1977).

14. McCormick, *Notes on Moral Theology,* pp. 737–745, gives a fair sampling of the initial responses and criticisms.

15. *Human Sexuality,* pp. 78–80.

16. Greeley, p. 143.

17. See David Hollenbach, S.J., *Claims in Conflict* (New York: Paulist Press, 1979); for the same phenomenon in the writings of the American bishops, cf. Overberg, *An Inconsistent Ethic?* pp. 171–187.

18. Burtchaell, p. 85.

19. *Human Sexuality,* p. 89.

20. David Reuben, M.D., *Everything You Always Wanted To Know About Sex* (New York: Bantam Books, 1971).

21. Preface, note 3.

22. Reuben, p. 124.

23. *Ibid.,* p. 77.

24. *Human Sexuality,* p. 81.

25. *Ibid.,* p. 82.

26. *Ibid.*

27. *Ibid.,* p. 83.

28. Bertocci, pp. 94–97.

29. *Human Sexuality,* p. 85

30. *Ibid.,* p. 86.

31. *Ibid.,* p. 91.

32. *Ibid.,* p. 95.

33. *Ibid.,* pp. 92–95.

34. *Ibid.,* p. 92.

35. *Ibid.,* p. 93.

36. *Ibid.*

37. *Ibid.,* p. 95.

38. *Ibid.*

39. William May and John Harvey, "On Understanding Human Sexuality: A Critique of the CTSA Study," *Communio* 4, No. 3 (Fall 1977), pp. 202, 211, 220; Richard Roach, "More Than Integration: The CTSA Report on Human Sexuality," *Communio* 5, No. 2 (Spring 1978), pp. 182–201.

40. McCormick, *Notes on Moral Theology 1965–1980,* p. 739; Daniel C. Maguire, "Of Sex and Ethical Methodology," Doherty (ed.), *Dimensions of Human Sexuality,* pp. 138–139.

41. Keane, pp. 57–70.

42. *Human Sexuality,* p. 228.

43. *Ibid.,* p. 227.

44. Betty Dodson, *Liberating Masturbation* (New York: Body-sex Designs, 1974).

45. *Human Sexuality,* p. 227.

46. *Ibid.,* p. 237.

47. *Ibid.,* p. 148.

48. Maguire, p. 136. See also Daniel C. Maguire, *The Moral*

Choice (Garden City: Doubleday, 1978), p. 162.

49. Anthony R. Kosnik, "Of Beginnings, Not Ends: A Rejoinder," *Dimensions of Human Sexuality,* pp. 215–216.

50. *Human Sexuality,* p. 169.

51. *Ibid.,* p. 187.

52. Boswell, pp. 207–266.

53. Martin S. Weinberg and Alan P. Bell (eds.), *Homosexuality: An Annotated Bibliography* (New York: Harper and Row, 1972); cited in *Human Sexuality,* p. 270, n. 147.

54. John J. McNeil, *The Church and the Homosexual* (Kansas City: Sheed Andrews and McMeel, Inc., 1976).

55. John Giles Milhaven, pp. 59–68; Charles E. Curran, "Dialogue with the Homophile Movement: The Morality of Homosexuality," *Catholic Moral Theology in Dialogue* (Notre Dame: Fides Publishers, 1972), pp. 184–219; more recently, "Moral Theology, Psychiatry and Homosexuality," *Transition and Tradition in Moral Theology* (Notre Dame: University of Notre Dame Press, 1979), pp. 59–80.

56. *Human Sexuality,* pp. 200–202.

57. *Ibid.,* pp. 206–209.

58. *Ibid.,* p. 203.

59. Maguire, *Dimensions of Human Sexuality,* pp. 132–134.

60. *Human Sexuality,* p. 204.

61. Donald Goergen, *The Sexual Celibate* (Evanston: The Seabury Press, 1975), continually avoids facing this point.

62. Germain Grisez, *Contraception and the Natural Law* (Milwaukee: Bruce, 1964), pp. 208–214, recognizes this clearly, however much he overstates the case.

63. Maguire, *Human Dimensions in Sexuality,* pp. 136–139; in the same volume, see the reply of Kosnik, pp. 215–216. Consequentialists often call deontological prohibitions products of untested intuition.

5
Other Revised Approaches

1. Sexuality as Language

In searching for more adequate ways to think about sexuality and morality, one of the more common convictions is that a law model of ethics or a code morality simply will not do. Such a model of ethics leads almost inevitably to a childish and primitive pattern of taboo morality, a morality that sees certain acts as forbidden apart from any consideration of intentions and circumstances. This is certainly the conviction of Andre Guindon, a conviction he defends at considerable length in the opening section of his book, *The Sexual Language*.[1] The insight behind this conviction is that moral actions cannot be simply identified with physical actions in sexual morality as well as any other area of morality. As Guindon himself expressed it:

> Human sexuality is not synonymous with genitality, and moral acts in this area should not be identified with merely biological functioning or physiological activity any more than they are in other areas of moral theology. The purely physical occurrence of genital stimulation to orgasm—

alone, through the agency of someone else, or with someone else in this or that fashion—is neither moral nor immoral. Before reference to a concrete moral agent is made,
morality or immorality can simply not be assessed in matters of sexuality.[2]

If a code morality specifying acts as right or wrong is not what
is needed, what, then, will take its place? Guindon's suggested candi-
date is meaning. In discussing the needs of young people, he declares,
"Youth need neither a 'realistic' nor an 'unrealistic' *code*. They need
significance. They need to be helped in discovering for themselves
what sexual meaning is and how to elaborate it creatively in their
own way of living it."[3] Unlike laws which deal with actions and can
be passed from one generation to the next, sexual meaning has to be
found anew, expressed and lived by each person. Sexual meaning
Guindon calls "an original human achievement."

How, then, do human beings learn and express meaning? They
learn to talk, they learn a language. It is Guindon's proposal, therefore, that sexual behavior should be regarded as a form of language,
as one basic way human beings have of saying what they mean, or, of
course, of misleading themselves and others. The authentic expression of meaning and the integrity of human communication would
then be the framework for evaluating the morality of sexual behavior. "The sexual language approach," writes Guindon, "fosters a
more adequate understanding of both sexual growth with its ups and
downs, and of the sexual project as a whole."[4]

The choice of language as a metaphor for understanding sexuality is by no means an arbitrary one. There is a profound link between
language and the human body, so much so that a recent popular
book could carry the readily understood title *Body Language*.[5] Guindon gives numerous examples of how the human body is so closely
tied to language, but his last example will best serve as an illustration
here. "No expression is more telling than this last one to summarize
what all other examples so strongly suggest: 'speaking' and 'keeping
in touch' are identified with each other in the daily experience of ordinary men and women."[6] Furthermore, this intimate link between
word and flesh[7] sets up the interplay between the spiritual and the
material, the mind and the body, the meaning and the medium used

to convey the meaning. This is the basis for understanding human sexuality as a language.

A few characteristics of language need to be noted here. As we learn a language, we establish a relationship between ourselves and our world; we find our place in the world. As we learn to speak the language, we also learn to express ourselves, to make known to others who we are and what we are about. For in speaking we always speak about ourselves to some extent, even when speaking about things. The meaning of language, we discover, develops out of the dialogue we share with other embodied persons. It emerges gradually out of the common interplay between people and with an open-ended or unfinished character to it. We may say all that we mean for the moment, but we will also mean more by what we say tomorrow. In sum, language is a social reality, a self-expressive reality, an interpersonal reality, an historical, developmental reality, that seeks inter-relationships and integration. Language seeks to make common sense.

Accordingly, Guindon sees sexuality in each person as "a requirement of body-spirit integration and social identity to be realized gradually through a long man-woman dialogue."[8] It calls for the integration within the self of sensuality and tenderness which is expressed in relationships of intimacy with other tender and sensuous selves. Sexual behavior, understood as language, speaks our own most personal and intimate experience of our bodily existence. In such speaking sexual meaning emerges and takes on a newness in the world, a certain originality. This will be the case unless our language (our sexual behavior) is nothing but the studied repetition of someone else's words. In the latter case the language soon becomes meaningless and sexuality loses its vitality. One is speaking a dead language.

This disintegration of language and of sexuality can take either the form of spiritualism or corporealism.[9] Spiritualism would prefer the word not to become flesh. Corporealism would prefer to have the flesh without the word. But in both cases the result is the same; sexuality loses its human meaning and becomes brutish, a point Rollo May was concerned to stress in *Love and Will*.[10] The general moral norm governing sexual behavior, therefore, could be expressed this way. Sexual behavior should be meaningful and truthful communication in one's specific life situation.

2. Truthful Sexual Expression

How Guindon applies this general understanding of sexual morality to specific issues may be illustrated here by his discussion of pre-marital sex,[11] though his book includes lengthy discussions of contraception, masturbation, sexual fantasies and homosexuality as well. What the unmarried heterosexual person is faced with as he or she becomes aware of being a sexed person attracted to other sexed persons is the specific task of learning the heterosexual language, of finding how to enter into the heterosexual dialogue. Sexual intercourse, which is the ultimate expression of physical and personal intimacy, is hardly the first word in the dialogue. However, "it might just be, logically, the first question to start with, because the answer one brings to it is decisive for the way one views the dating pattern."[12]

The most common arguments in favor of pre-marital sexual intercourse outside a context of personal love can be reduced to three forms. The first form of argument sees sex as fun. It makes one feel good or more alive or more relaxed or more with it. What could be wrong with that! Guindon has but one comment to offer such arguments: "Those who really need coitus to feel alive or dispel ignorance are confined to the sub-human world of skin-level knowledge: such a world is a tragedy."[13] The other two arguments he takes more seriously. One argument seeks to avoid a harm—abstention from coitus by people who face a prolonged adolescence imposes an unnatural strain on young people and leads to sexual repressions and inhibitions. The other argument seeks a positive benefit—the experience of pre-marital intercourse is beneficial, perhaps even essential, for successful sexual adjustment in marriage.

The empirical evidence to support either of these claims is indecisive; as much evidence can be marshaled in rebuttal as in support. More to the point, however, both arguments view human sexuality as something less than fully human. "It is possible," contends Guindon, "for human beings to control their drives rationally, consciously and purposefully."[14] Indeed, the inability to do so is a sign of personal and cultural bankruptcy. Furthermore, human beings do not learn personal sexual adjustment to one another by relating to third parties. The adjustment is one of persons, not bodies. Therefore sexual intercourse between two people who are not committed to one another "is a disintegrative use of the sexual language."[15]

But what of pre-marital sex "with love"? Since in Guindon's understanding the authentic language that sexual intercourse speaks is the language of love and personal intimacy, can there be any kind of moral objection to this kind of sexual behavior? For a variety of converging reasons he finds it generally[16] objectionable. But the major reason has to do with the understanding of sexual behavior as language:

> Any sexual caress among humans is a speaking thing: it discloses to the other the intention and the very being of its author. Man expresses his own fruition carnally; and, conversely, that expression makes him to exist in a new way. . . . This is in fact the most fundamental postulate of all ethics; there is not one realization, expressive of man's being, which does not contribute to his own regeneration, or, inversely, to his downfall.[17]

Now sexual expression, like all human language, does not mean just anything the individual wants it to mean. Sexual intercourse says something rather specific; it speaks a two-in-one flesh unity, a bonding, a coupling between the two people. "If the carnal gestures of love have any meaning, surely this is what they signify. . . . The words simply spell out what the bodies themselves say."[18]

Such sexual expression, before the personal and public determination to become and be a couple, is not, generally, a true statement. Too often, says Guindon, such sexual expression is an obstacle to a developing love, not an expression enriching personal love. The two lovers grow in love not with one another but with love-making.[19] They fall into the spiritual trap that haunts all mystics: to take the gifts of divine love for the giver of those gifts. To the extent that such sexual expression is a lie, it is destructive to both parties. And the gravity of such a moral failing would be determined not by the nature of the act, but by its degree of inauthenticity.

Guindon's approach to sexual ethics is certainly suggestive. It has been found perceptive and helpful in unfolding the human meaning of sexuality even by some of his critics. But he has been faulted for what might be called an intuitive and highly personal method of moral analysis, which the approach through language almost certainly entails. Such an approach is not wrong but needs to be complemented by more precise methods. As William May commented in his review of Guindon's book, it is marred "above all by a failure to provide a genuine moral methodology for discussing the meaning of human acts. He hints at such a methodology but leaves its precise nature vague and unspecified."[20]

The demand for a better methodology might well be regarded as a subtle return to code morality and absolute rules. But that is not necessarily so. One school[21] of theologians has proposed a method of ethical analysis that is more exact and controlled without being legalistic. Philip Keane has employed this method in *Sexual Morality: A Catholic Perspective*. The method has two fundamental ideas: the notion of fundamental option and the distinction between ontic and moral evil, and we will start with them.

3. Fundamental Option

Contemporary biblical scholarship has helped us recognize anew that conversion is the central moral message of the Gospel, as Charles Curran has put it.[22] Jesus' fundamental demand, as expressed in Mark's Gospel (1:15), is to "repent and believe in the good news." This experience of conversion has two poles, repentance and belief, which are not two separate moments but correlative aspects of the same moment or experience. Biblical language expresses this symbolically in a variety of ways. It is a death and a rebirth, a turning away from the darkness to the light, a putting off of the old man and putting on the new, a dying with Christ to rise with him. The Old Testament description of God's word as a two-edged sword, as a word which judges and condemns us as sinners but at the same time is a word of mercy and promise, affords the same insight.

This two-sided character of conversion can also be illustrated through the example of biblical individuals who encounter God or who are awakened to a consciousness of divine or transcendent reality. The experience of Peter as recounted in Luke's Gospel (5:13) will serve as one example. After a fruitless night of fishing it is the miraculous catch of fish which awakens Peter's consciousness to an awareness that there is more to Jesus than meets the eye. He find himself in the presence of someone who elicits from him that most natural gesture of awe and reverence—he falls to his knees—and the confession of his own sin and unworthiness: "Depart from me, O Lord, for I am a sinful man."

But the story does not end with confession. Immediately a new life, a new possibility, is held out to Peter. He is summoned to leave his old life behind and to follow Jesus. He is called upon to make a basic choice, a fundamental option, to turn away from one life direction and point himself in another. The result of this choice is a fundamental stance, as Timothy O'Connell has called it, a stance of faith and trust in and love for Jesus.[23] Peter has been converted.

This conversion implies a new awareness of God, a new awareness of the self, and a new awareness of the relationship between God and the self and between the self and others. It calls for an inner reorientation and integration of the self. As Keane puts it, "The term 'fundamental option' means the stable orientation or life direction that exists at the core level of the human person."[24] Effected by grace it is this stable orientation which constitutes our relationship to or against God. Ethically it is a stable orientation toward the good or toward evil. A stable orientation toward God and the good would be what was traditionally meant by being in the state of grace. A core orientation against God and the good would constitute the state of mortal sin.

If we again take our lead from the example of Peter, we see that this inner orientation of the self finds expression in particular actions, actions which rarely, if ever, give full and accurate expression to the inner orientation or fundamental option. In the fullness of his enthusiasm Peter wanted to keep Jesus from the cross, by a sword if necessary. He was rebuked for such attempts, but they did not destroy his fundamental orientation. In the weakness of his flesh he fell asleep in the garden and denied knowing Jesus three times. He wept and lamented such acts but they only imperiled, they did not destroy, his fundamental option.

The importance of this idea for morality is laid out clearly by Keane.

> What we must do in assessing the presence or absence of sin is to look to the whole person so as to grasp what the person is like on the core level of his or her being. To see the whole person, to see the core or heart of a person, we should take into account the entire pattern of a person's actions. We should look to a series of actions emerging from the person rather than to any one act alone.[25]

Consequently, the morality and the gravity of any action have to be assessed not merely in terms of what the action itself is, but in the context of a pattern of life, in reference to the fundamental option. The fundamental option itself is, of course, known with certainty only to God. But this way of understanding human beings points out the real importance of our moral choices and our struggles to know what is good and what is evil. For our choices either affirm and strengthen our fundamental option for God or they weaken and destroy it. It is only in and through our particular choices of good and evil that we orient ourselves more fully to or away from God. Conversion becomes a continuous process and the question of concrete moral good and evil a crucial one.

4. Moral and Ontic Good and Evil

Since the most fundamental moral obligation which all human beings have is to love and do the good and to avoid evil, the categories of good and evil should receive priority in moral thought, and they do so in Keane's approach. Yet in order to understand what is morally good and evil, it is first necessary to make a distinction between pre-moral or physical or ontic good and evil and moral good and evil. Keane himself prefers the term "ontic evil" for purposes of simplicity,[26] and we will follow his lead here.

Basic to an understanding of this distinction is the recognition of the existence of real objective goods and evils in the world, which things are to be understood as ontic goods or evils because there is as yet no question of the relationship of a human will to them in a particular set of circumstances. For example, life is an ontic good; cancer is an ontic evil. If it should be objected that all goods are relational, are good only for someone or something under some particular aspect, and are not simply good in themselves apart from such relations, the point is readily conceded. For the only perspective from which human beings can call anything good is that they recognize that it meets a human need or desire, or more precisely that it has the capacity to do so. Once it is clear that that is the perspective, however, it is also the case that the reality called good does, in fact, have the intrinsic qualities which enable it to meet the need or desire.

Life is one such basic good, for it is the essential pre-condition for the experiencing of all other goods. So life is properly valued. It is a good not merely because people declare it to be good, or psychologically find that it is a wonderful thing to be alive—many people do not—but because life of its very nature is the essential condition for any experience of the good at all. Life, of course, is also the essential condition for experiencing evils, including that penultimate evil, death. But that does not make life equally an ontic good and evil. Life alone has the capaicty to be good for human beings. Death, of its very nature, is the end of human being and the end of all experience of goods. As such it is never a good for human beings and can never be welcomed as a good, though it can obviously be welcomed as an end when one is at the end. But it always remains, at best, the lesser of two evils.

Given the existence of ontic goods and evils, the meaning of moral good and evil can be expressed. Moral evil consists in willingly to allow or cause an ontic evil to occur in the world unnecessarily or without a proportionate reason. A morally good act would be one for which there was a proportionate reason. For there is a second recognition involved here. As Keane states the matter, "It can be said that no human act ever actualizes the fullness of human possibility. All human acts contain within themselves elements of non-good."[27] Some of these minor non-goods are almost negligible, but some are quite significant. For instance, the decision to read this book means inevitably that the reader will forego the realization of other goods— some much needed relaxation, perhaps, or some badly needed exercise, or some private time to spend with a loved one. Consequently, all human choices inescapably involve one in turning away from one good to prefer another. What makes a choice morally good is the presence, in the total concrete context of the choice, of a proportionate reason. The absence of a proportionate reason would make the choice morally evil.[28]

5. Application to Sexual Morality

When this method of ethical analysis is applied to sexual morality, the first task is to specify the ontic goods associated with sexuality. As we have seen, the primary goods associated with sexuality in the Christian tradition were the procreative good of children and the unitive good of the loving communion of the sexual partners. The good of sensual pleasure was not seen as an autonomous human good, but as one that had to be associated with love. To illustrate briefly Keane's application of the method, we may take his discussion of artificial contraception.[29]

The use of contraceptive methods of birth control always involves ontic evil for two reasons: "their non-openness to procreation in individual acts and ... problems with the various birth control methods,"[30] by which Keane means the various physical and psychological side effects. He reads *Humanae Vitae,* therefore, as "stating the most ideal human possibility for intercourse."[31] Could there ever be a proportionate reason for allowing or causing these ontic evils to exist in the world, so that the ontic evil of contraceptive intercourse would not be a moral evil as well? Keane's answer is yes, a yes which depends on two factors. One is the good of sexual communion. A prolonged abstention from sexual relations means that the couple foregoes the increase of their unity and love arising from the giving, receiving and sharing of physical pleasure and intimacy—an ontic evil. The second factor is the proportionate reason which is to be found in the concrete circumstances of the couple. As he explains the whole matter:

> If a couple face serious medical, psychological, or economic problems, their need for the human values involved in sexual communion would seem to give moral justification to their use of birth control devices. Such a decision will be undertaken with some regret (due to the ontically evil ele-

ments of birth control), but with a good conscience and with the conviction that, all things being considered, their action is objectively moral.[32]

This mode of moral analysis does not allow the conclusion that any sexual act is always and everywhere morally wrong. It does, however, allow for the formulation of virtually exceptionless rules that would prohibit certain actions for all practical purposes. These rules emerge because "there are some actions in which the ontic evil is so predominant that it is virtually impossible for us humans to conceive of concrete cases where there might be anything related to the concreteness of the act that would justify it morally."[33] As examples in the sexual area, Keane mentions rape and incest. A substantial objection, however, has been made to this method of analysis by some theologians persuaded of the correctness of the traditional position. Their appeal is not simply to the authority of the Pope and the tradition, but to a more accurate understanding of the relationship of the human person to ontic good and evil. Therefore this chapter appropriately concludes with an examination of their position.

6. Fundamental Human Goods

The method of ethical analysis, and its subsequent application to sexual behaviors, which we are going to examine next, was developed in some detail by Germain Grisez in his book *Contraception and the Natural Law,* published in 1964. He did not claim originality for it, only that it was a more accurate reading of Thomas Aquinas. He further developed the method in its theoretical form in a book he co-authored with Russell Shaw in 1974, *Beyond the New Morality.*[34] Most recently he has applied the method to the question of euthanasia in cooperation with Joseph Boyle.[35] That basic approach to understanding moral questions has been adapted to his own work by William E. May in his book, *Becoming Human: An Invitation to Christian Ethics.* May explicitly acknowledges Grisez and Paul Ramsey as "the very best living analysts of moral action writing in English."[36] Most recently, Robert Joyce has adopted this ethical approach in *Human Sexual Ecology.*[37] In this book, which is an extensive and uncritical defense of the rightness and goodness of natural family planning, Joyce comments on his debt to both Grisez and May.[38]

There are at least three good reasons for giving serious attention to the ethical approach and arguments of these authors. First of all, their conclusions in the matter of sexual practices are the same as those of the official teaching of the Catholic Church in regard to sexual morality. That is not a fact that can weigh lightly on the Catholic conscience. But unlike many authors who simply invoke the Church's teaching authority to support their conclusions, these authors argue the issues on their own merits. That is to say, they are writing about sexuality and morality, not about the obedience due to authoritative papal and episcopal documents. A second reason for giving them serious attention is that their approach is truly distinctive and sophisticated. Indeed, their sophistication will pose a problem for us here in trying to give a clear and uncomplicated explanation of it. But the primary place that their approach gives to the human obligation to do the good, and not simply avoid evil, demands that we at least try to understand them.

There is also a third, if somewhat oblique, reason for giving serious attention to the views of these men. One of the more frequent complaints that people level at the official teaching of the Church on sexual morality is that it is the product of male celibates who have no personal experience of what they are talking about. Whatever the merits of that criticism may be, the men whose views we are going to consider are all married laymen with families, and ostensibly they know of what they speak. At least two of them work in close collaboration with their wives and have consciously offered explicit witness that the teachings they espouse and defend are personally meaningful and possible.[39] Of course their personal experience of marriage and family no more guarantees the truth of their views than the Pope's celibate experience means that his teachings are wrong. But the charge that the Church's official teaching on sexuality is largely the result of a repressed celibate fear of sex simply will not stand.

The approach to moral questions adopted by these authors can be unfolded through four considerations. First, the basic human obligation is to be, just as the basic question is to be or not to be. The obligation is to be what we are to the fullest degree possible, to be fully *human*. More concretely this means that human beings, to be human, ought to be fully free and rational, fully social, and fully open to the transcendent horizon of all human being which religious believers call the mystery of God. If that is the fundamental human obligation, immorality will then be seen as a form of self-negation or self-contradiction. As Grisez and Russell express it:

> When we say that something is immoral, we are saying that it is a kind of self-mutilation, that it represents irrationality in action, that it is a violation (at least incipient) of community, and that it is a rejection of God (or the transcendent Other).[40]

In short, moral evil is understood to be the refusal to realize the good to which we are called, to the degree it is possible for each of us to do so. Moral evil does not consist in doing bad things so much as it consists in the refusal to do the good of which we are capable.

The second consideration focuses on the good which we are called to do. Undoubtedly there is an inexhaustible list of good things for human beings to do, an almost infinite number of values to realize in their lives. But, based upon the inherent tendencies of all human beings, Grisez proposed eight goods as basic or fundamental human goods.[41] These goods can also be labeled purposes, ends, or goals. Four of them are substantive purposes, values to be directly sought for their own sake: life, play, aesthetic experience, speculative knowledge. Four of them are reflexive purposes, values that are essential, accompanying aspects of all activity: integrity, authenticity, friendship, religion. All other goods, values or purposes are simply specifications or extensions of these basic human goods. Because these are basic human goods, and because our fundamental obligation is to realize the good in our lives, a specific moral norm emerges, which also leads to a third consideration. We should never directly choose against a fundamental good of human personhood; to do so is intrinsically wrong and always immoral.

Everyone recognizes the impossibility of realizing all human goods, all human potentialities in any one way of life, no less than in any one choice. To choose one good always means that we forego other goods, don't realize other potentialities. Such choices, however, can be made with one of two attitudes. There is an inclusive attitude which continues to recognize and be open to the goods which one has deliberately not chosen to realize here and now in this choice, or there is an exclusive attitude which denies the goodness of the values rejected and closes the self off to the goods one has not chosen to realize here and now. A simple example can make the difference clearer. A person may choose the life of conjugal love and sexual friendship even while recognizing the goodness of a life of committed celibacy for the sake of the kingdom of God and remaining open to the truth and wisdom to be learned from those who have chosen such a life. Or he or she can choose marriage because the celibate life of commitment appears as lonely, frustrating, and unworthy of human love. Therefore, in regard to the fundamental goods of human personhood, our choices should be inclusive, not exclusive.[42] Otherwise we deny the possibility of our human fulfillment.

The fourth consideration is the most difficult to express clearly. It has to do with how one realizes the good which is the object of one's choice. It may be best, therefore, to proceed as concretely as possible. For that reason, in developing this final consideration, we will do so by applying it and the other three considerations to the question of the morality of contraceptive intercourse. For it is not simply a question of having an inclusive attitude or a correct intention behind our choices. Human beings realize the good in action, not simply in having good intentions. What is required, therefore, is what William May has called "an ethics of intent + content."[43]

If the primary goods specifically associated with sexuality are life and love—friendship in the language of Grisez's listing of basic goods[44]—then we should never deliberately choose against either one, even while recognizing that it is not always humanly possible to realize both goods. But being open to life and love is not simply a matter of attitude. It also involves what we do. The moral good is not realized in our lives as a product or consequence of our good intentions that is extrinsic to our action. It is realized in our lives by way of participation or sharing. A couple realizes the value of mutual love, among other ways, by participating in the reality of mutual love-making. The good they realize is not a consequence external to their action, but something they participate in, while they do what they do. This explains, by way of illustration, why rape is always wrong, even if it should lead to some unimaginable good consequences. The act itself, no matter what the consequences, or the intention of the agent, fails to realize the values possible in sexual intercourse. It simply excludes, by the very nature of the act, the good of love. It is not and cannot ever be an act of sharing—of giving and receiving, but only taking and getting. It can never be a human act and so it is intrinsically disordered and always wrong.

In a comparable way, contraceptive intercourse is viewed as an act that turns against a basic value of human personhood—life. Unlike natural family planning, which is an inclusive choice, artificial contraception deliberately excludes the value of life. It fails to realize the fullness of human possibility, not because of human finitude or the limits of nature and history, but because of deliberate human choice and action. The couple chooses deliberately to be less than they could be, and so the action is intrinsically disordered and always immoral. That is what these writers mean by immorality. Or as Grisez and Shaw summarize the matter:

> This is the paradox—the irrationality in action—of exclusivistic choice. . . . One sets out to make a free choice, to exercise self-determination; one ends up pursuing a particular objective, his action now merely a matter of doing as he pleases. Instead of realizing himself by remaining open to fuller personhood, the person choosing exclusivistically makes even that aspect of himself that is fulfilled by his choice into a definite and limited objective, which is now *extrinsic* to the very center of his personhood. Choosing exclusivistically, one moves *from being* a person *to having* something one happens to want.[44]

To be fully clear and persuasive, this understanding of morality would need a more ample defense than can be offered here. But one positive and one negative comment may be made by way of conclusion. Whatever the merit of their conclusions on particular acts, these authors made it clear that the moral imperative of our human existence is a dynamic demand for the fullness of human personhood. Morality cannot be framed as a set of minimal obligations or duties. To be deliberately and purposefully less than a person, less free, less rational, less loving than one could really be, is to fail oneself, one's neighbors, one's God. Such a view can easily be idealized and made to sound utopian and completely out of touch with reality, but it need not be.

On the other hand, while the idea that we realize values by sharing or participating in them and not by possessing them is quite true, the authors seem to work with a very abstract notion of values or good. This is particularly true in regard to the value of life, and it is this abstract quality which seems to cause so much confusion in the birth control discussion. For the life that the married couple is being asked to remain open to is not life in general but the concrete living human person that may well be the fruit of their love-making. While I know of no Catholic author who would not acknowledge the value of this child so conceived, whether wanted intentionally or not, I know of no author who therefore insists that the fullness of value demands that the couple produce as many children as they possibly can. It still remains unclear, therefore, why an inclusive choice of the basic goods of human life requires that every act of sexual intercourse must be open to the abstract value of life but not to the possibility of a concrete loving human being. This seems to be not a mystery, but simple mystification.

Notes

1. Guindon, pp. 7–51.

2. *Ibid.,* pp. 27–28.

3. *Ibid.,* p. 36.

4. *Ibid.,* p. 83.

5. Julius Fast, *Body Language* (New York: M. Evans, 1977).

6. Guindon, p. 85.

7. A specific reference to Jn 1:14, "and the Word became flesh and dwelt among us," is intended.

8. Guindon, p. 87.

9. *Ibid.,* pp. 90–106.

10. R. May, pp. 45–48.

11. Guindon, pp. 379–439.

12. *Ibid.,* p. 383.

13. *Ibid.,* pp. 384–385.

14. *Ibid.,* p. 386.

15. *Ibid.,* p. 413.

16. The reader should note the word "generally," as opposed to "always" or "absolutely," or even "virtually always."

17. Guindon, p. 413.

18. *Ibid.,* p. 423.

19. *Ibid.,* p. 424.

20. William E. May, "Review of *The Sexual Language,*" *Horizons* 5, No. 1 (Spring 1978), p. 131.

21. It is not strictly accurate to call them a school, but they have been in common dialogue with one another. See Curran and McCormick (eds.), *Readings in Moral Theology No. 1.*

22. Charles E. Curran, *A New Look at Christian Morality* (Notre Dame: Fides, 1968), p. 25; James P. Hanigan, "The Marcan Concept of the Christian Life," *Homiletic and Pastoral Review* LXVII, 10 (July 1967), pp. 839–848.

23. Timothy O'Connell, *Principles for a Catholic Morality* (New York: Seabury Press, 1978), pp. 64–66.

24. Keane, p. 38.

25. *Ibid.,* p. 37.

26. *Ibid.,* p. 40, p. 200 n. 36.

27. *Ibid.,* p. 47.

28. *Ibid.,* pp. 47–51.

29. *Ibid.,* pp. 121–134.

30. *Ibid.,* p. 124.

31. *Ibid.,* p. 125.

32. *Ibid.*

33. *Ibid.,* pp. 50–51.

34. Germain Grisez and Russell Shaw, *Beyond the New Morality: The Responsibilities of Freedom* (Notre Dame: University of Notre Dame Press, 1974).

35. Germain Grisez and Joseph M. Boyle, Jr., *Life and Death with Liberty and Justice* (Notre Dame: University of Notre Dame Press, 1979). See also Germain Grisez, *Abortion: The Myths, The Realities and The Arguments* (New York: Corpus, 1970).

36. William E. May, *Becoming Human: An Invitation to Chris-*

tian Ethics (Dayton: Pflaum, 1975), p. 146; see also William E. May, "An Integrist Understanding," in Doherty (ed.), *Dimensions of Human Sexuality*, pp. 95–124.

37. Robert E. Joyce, *Human Sexual Ecology: A Philosophy and Ethics of Man and Woman* (Washington, D.C.: University Press of America, 1981).

38. *Ibid.,* p. xiv.

39. Grisez, *Contraception and the Natural Law,* pp. 14–15, Joyce, p. xv, and the jointly written work by Mary Rosera Joyce and Robert E. Joyce, *New Dynamics in Sexual Love: A Revolutionary Approach to Marriage and Celibacy* (Collegeville: St. John's University Press, 1970).

40. Grisez and Shaw, p. 92.

41. *Ibid.,* pp. 64–74; Joyce, pp. 161–174.

42. Grisez and Shaw, pp. 85–95.

43. W. May, *Becoming Human,* p. 83.

44. Grisez and Shaw, pp. 94–95.

6
New Directions for Sexual Morality

Having reviewed traditional and contemporary efforts to think about sexuality and morality, are there any clear achievements and any signs of new directions and new possibilities? The achievements are more visible and easier to recount. The new directions are more a matter for speculation and hope. Despite the often heated controversies over sexual morality among contemporary Christian theologians, a significant degree of consensus appears to have been reached which deserves to be noted and appreciated. This consensus which has been achieved seems to center around four areas: the fundamental importance of sexuality, its necessary connection with personal love, its dynamic orientation to intimacy, and its social importance in regard to life. These points of agreement, and the as yet unclarified issues connected with them, may well indicate the future agenda for Christian sexual morality.

1. The Fundamental Importance of Sexuality

While the simple identification of morality with sexual conduct was undoubtedly a mistake, it is clear that sexual behavior divorced from a moral context can only lead to tragedy. In Rollo May's language, sexual behavior separated from human willing and love is a personal psychological and social disaster.[1] Sexuality is too important to human wholeness to be treated either as a joke or as a casual satisfaction of a physical need. It is also too important to be ignored or repressed. As Richard McBrien among others has pointed out, "a denial or repression of our sexuality entails also a repression of sensitivity, warmth, openness and mutual respect in interpersonal relationships."[2] What is unique about human sexuality, in contrast to animal sexuality, is that human beings are hyper-sexual. They are not dependent on their instincts and natural biological rhythms for sexual arousal and performance. Accordingly sexuality is a much larger factor in human life than in animal life and much more important to human well-being than to animal well-being. Human beings need to become more, not less, sexual.

All the authors discussed in the previous pages give at least lip service to this basic truth, and there is no good reason to believe that they are not at least trying to take it seriously. When Pope John Paul II talks about "the mystical meaning of the body," when Archbishop Bernardin calls for a positive doctrine of sexuality,[3] when theologians stress the basic goodness of sexuality, they are all recognizing the fundamental importance of sexuality to human personal and social well-being. The way people conduct themselves sexually is not seen by any of them as a matter of indifference or of little moment. The recognition of the importance of sexuality has immediate consequences for morality, and this, too, is a matter of common agreement. Sexual morality cannot be reduced to a calculus of pain and pleasure, or governed by the norm that anything is acceptable if it is mutually agreeable, without depersonalizing human beings. Nor can a doctrine of sexuality be expounded in and confined to a list of do's and don'ts, though the precise place for and nature of moral rules in sexual morality is still a question of debate.[4]

Germain Grisez's formulation of the matter is as helpful as any. The human values of sexuality are not realized as something extrinsic to sexual actions. They are realized by way of participation in these values, in the course of doing the actions. This is an important point and deserves further clarification.

All human actions can be considered in one of three ways: as labor, as work, or as action.[5] The distinguishing feature of labor is that it is an activity performed under the demand of necessity, of some kind of compulsion. The only form of freedom required to do it is physical freedom, the freedom of bodily movement. The slave in the field picking the crops at his owner's behest has no say in the matter. The teenager, compulsively masturbating, is in the same situation. The activity of both is properly described as labor. And the only point or purpose to labor, for the one laboring, the only end or good being sought, is to get the action over and done with. Labor is patently dehumanizing, a fact we finally recognized in abolishing slavery. Not all labor is immoral, but it is clearly immoral when we can do something about abolishing the necessity but either will not or do not.

Human beings also work. What distinguishes work from labor is that the worker chooses the ends for which he or she will work. The worker's purpose is his or her own. Therefore the kind of freedom the worker needs is freedom of choice as well as bodily freedom, the freedom to decide the purposes or goods one will seek as the fruit of one's efforts. The slave in the fields, once released from slavery, may then decide to work in the fields for wages. The compulsive masturbator, once free of the compulsion, may decide to masturbate for the feeling of pleasure or sexual release the act affords him or her. But in any case, it is not the work itself which is of interest to the worker but the product of the work, its result or consequence. The work has a purely instrumental or utilitarian value.

Work is less dehumanizing than labor, for the worker has the choice of ends and so exercises greater freedom than the laborer. But in giving his activity away for the sake of an end extrinsic to the act, the worker is alienated from his own activity. He reduces what is his own—his work—to a means to an end. This might be clearer in the case of the ex-slave working for wages than in the case of the teenager masturbating for pleasure. The ex-slave sells his work. On reflection, however, it is clear that the teenager is using his body as a means. He is not being his body. Work is, of course, not always immoral, even when it is not fully human. But we do recognize the obligation in justice to our own humanity to make work and the conditions in which we work more humane. The criteria of efficiency and utility are appropriate criteria for evaluating work, but they are not the only considerations, since people are not machines. To refuse to make work more human when we can and to the degree we can is immoral.

Finally human activity can also be regarded as action. Action is distinguished from labor because it is freely chosen for the sake of the activity itself and not for some end the activity will achieve. Whereas the worker values the product of his work, the actor values acting and realizes the value in the experience of acting. The ex-slave may take to the fields simply because he enjoys the fresh air, the smells of the crops, the experience of bending and lifting and being busy. The kind of freedom involved in acting is not merely bodily freedom and freedom of choice, but the freedom of self-determination. The human person determines himself or herself only in acting, not in labor, not in work. It is hard to see how masturbation could ever take on the fully human meaning of action.

Two additional points need to be made about the way of understanding the morality of human acts. One thing that determines whether a particular activity counts as labor, work, or action is the perspective or attitude of the agent. The slave in the field, by a change of perspective, can give his labor features of action. When Paul told new Christians who were slaves to obey their masters as though they were obeying Christ, he was adding a humanizing aspect to their labor. Many people who work for a living also relish the activity they perform, and their work is also action. People who play sports for a living might be good examples of this. But a simple change of attitude or perspective does not make the slave's activity cease to be labor or the worker's activity cease to be work. No mere intention can effect that. Only a change in the social conditions of the world, a change in reality and not merely in the inner self, can bring that about.

Because all of us have needs that must be met if we are to survive, there is always a horizon of labor about what we do. Because most of us must work for a living, there is always an aspect of labor about our work. In affirming that it is only in action that we are able to be self-determining and fully human, we do not deny either the necessity of labor or the real values of work and the products of work. But the affirmation does recognize that there is more to human activity and to justice and right, and so to morality, than either necessity (law) or a simple calculation of results (consequences) can account for. The relationship that exists between the means (our activity) and the end (the good sought) is not a single relationship but a plural one. Consequently, where some measure of self-determination, some opportunity for participating in value in the very process of acting, is not available, then the act is inevitably dehumanizing or contrary to the nature of the human person. In technical ethical terms this is to recognize deontological characteristics in morality as well as consequentialist ones.[6]

One of the still unresolved issues in morality is the precise way of relating the deontological and consequentialist features of sexual acts, and so whether moral rules bind generally or absolutely, are replete with exceptions or are virtually exceptionless. We can expect this debate to continue. But at least one important agreement emerges out of this whole discussion—there is a central place in sexual morality for the virtue of chastity, and for the free, rational expression of one's sexuality, if it is to be a truly human expression. Christian sexual morality is not prudish, but neither is it hedonistic and self-indulgent. It does, and with continued unanimity, insist on chastity—not just anything goes.

2. Sex and Personal Love

After centuries of talking about procreation as the primary purpose of human sexuality, there is a growing consensus that sexuality finds its primary significance in inter-personal love. The one notable exception to this consensus is, unfortunately, the Vatican Congregation for the Doctrine of Faith, which still insists that even Vatican II taught that procreation was the primary purpose.[7] To recognize that the Vatican Congregation's response is not merely reactionary, however, and to appreciate the significance of the stress on inter-personal love, several considerations are necessary. In our evaluation of the book *Human Sexuality,* it was pointed out that the value-criteria used to evaluate sexual behavior were not sex-specific. They applied equally well to behaviors that were not explicitly sexual. But why should this be a problem?

The fundamental commandment issued to followers of Jesus Christ is that they are to love one another as he has loved them. All their behaviors are to have their primary significance as expressions of love. All their relationships are to be relationships of love. This is not unique to sexual relationships. Yet surely there is something specifically different about the love a teacher has and expresses to his students and the love that same teacher has and expresses to his wife. It might well be an expression of love for his students if the teacher insists on a weekly quiz on the material in his class lectures. But most people would look askance at the husband who insisted that his wife take a weekly quiz on the material in his dinner table conversation. Different relationships have different specific criteria to guide them. What criteria should guide the explicitly sexual relationship? The Vatican Congregation continues to insist that the education and rearing of children should.

A second consideration is that in many parts of the world even today, and certainly in the past, marriage was entered into for the precise purpose of procreation, even while the motives for wanting children were various. Love was not necessarily a factor and rarely an important one. In associating sexuality with marriage, the Church made love a dimension of both the marital relationship and the sexual relationship. In the process love took on a new meaning and a new importance which has led theologians to find the primary meaning of sexual expression in inter-personal love.

A third consideration has to do with the excessively romantic and sentimentalized notion of love so prevalent in American popular culture. It is a notion of love which seems to equate love with strong sexual feelings or warm emotional feelings. In this cultural context sexual behavior becomes a way of expressing those feelings. Sex with affection or caring sex becomes acceptable and love comes to mean the manipulation of feelings, either one's own or another's. One might well hesitate to say that sexuality finds its primary meaning in inter-personal love, given such a chance of cultural misunderstanding.

Yet it is being said, and for good reason. The task of our sexuality is to relate us to others. To enter into explicitly sexual relationships involving the expression of erotic feelings and acts is to enter into inter-personal relationships. Such relationships have an integrity and sustain their authenticity only to the degree that a sharing of persons takes place. A teacher's relationship with his students, albeit a relationship of love, is not an inter-personal relationship, at least not directly so. And the direct personal relationship finds its meaning in a bonding of love whose symbolic expression is the two-in-one flesh unity of sexual intercourse. The act of sexual intercourse is a complete sharing of two bodily persons, one with the other. People do it humanly and morally only because they love one another in a rather special and unique way, as partners, as life-sharers. And so this love calls for the institution of marriage.

To be as clear as possible a further word is called for. The Christian understanding of love is that it is first something persons do; only secondarily is it to be understood as a state or a condition, as something that happens to a person, as in "being in love." God, the eternal lover who is love, loves human beings in his trinitarian activity of creation, redemption, and sanctification. His is not a passive "being in love." God's love for us is ultimately what makes it possible for us to love one another. But human love, too, is active; it calls for personal commitment, a fact that all who love and are loved know. Even those who marry, planning to divorce should the marriage not work out, or who live together before marriage to test whether they really are compatible and really do love one another, know that inter-personal love is forever. What they do not seem to realize is that human love is active, something one does. And it is manifestly impossible to share one's entire person with another if you are not willing to share your history, your past, present and future, with that person. This leads us to the dynamics of sexuality toward intimacy.

3. Dynamic Toward Intimacy

In his *New Agenda* for theology in the modern world, Andrew Greeley argued that the urgent question sexual morality had to ask was: "How do people grow in intimacy one with the other? In particular, how can two people who are committed to genital union with each other grow in their physical and psychological love?"[8] How do two people who are committed to the two-in-one flesh unity of marriage sustain and deepen that unity, even while they continue to grow and develop individually as persons? For increased intimacy is the dynamic of human sexuality, and, properly understood, is the dynamic that urges sexual love to be fruitful if it is to remain authentic.

On this point, too, there is a growing consensus, but not on all its particular demands and consequences.

That the human sexual drive moves us to seek physical intimacy is clear to everyone who ever went out on a date with a person he or she found attractive. As Guindon made clear in his discussion of language, human beings are moved to keep in touch, and the closer their relationship, the more in touch they want to keep. Yet many human efforts at intimacy, at filling up the loneliness of human existence for which God gave Adam and Eve to one another, come to naught or prove highly unsatisfactory. A sexual morality that is both truly about sex and is itself moral must be one that both promotes and safeguards intimacy. The common concern for responsible parenthood reflects this, for however great a blessing children may be in a marriage, they can put a strain on personal intimacy.

There are many factors in human experience that hinder, strain and even destroy intimacy. Some are due simply to human finitude. People get tired, distracted, sick. The range of their interests is limited. Try as they might, they simply cannot get interested in opera, or sports, or economic theory. Some factors are due to human sinfulness, both personal and social. People get angry or annoyed, judge rashly, act selfishly, and make unreasonable demands on others' time and energy. The sacrament of reconciliation becomes essential to intimate relationships. Inflation, tax rates, job, joblessness, and, most terribly, crime and war wreak havoc with intimate relationships. The American bishops' concern with the well-being of the family has led them inevitably into economic and political issues.[9]

The traditional prohibitions regarding sexual conduct were designed to protect intimacy, if not to foster and strengthen it. Certainly adultery is a threat to an intimate relationship, and divorce puts an end to such a relationship. Solitary sexual practices were forbidden, at least in part, because they are solitary, whereas the human meaning of sexuality is relational. But prohibitions, while they may protect against what threatens intimacy, do not reveal how intimacy can be fostered and strengthened. That sexual morality must serve human intimacy is a matter of consensus, even while the practical implications of that consensus remain a matter of some dispute, as do the disagreements over the morality of homosexual relationships, pre-marital sex and artificial contraception attest.

These three sexual issues receive great attention today, in part because of their ambiguous relationship to the growth of human intimacy. It seems clear, for example, to Robert Joyce that natural family planning, involving the mutual responsibility and concern of husband and wife, actually enhances the intimacy of the couple, while authors like Curran and Keane find the good of human intimacy a sufficient reason for tolerating contraceptive intercourse in some cases. An author like Andre Guindon thinks that pre-marital sex between a couple in love generally hurts their developing intimacy, while the authors of *Human Sexuality* are much less certain of this. The tolerance of stable homosexual relationships by Maguire, McNeil and others is, in part, because they see sexual expression in these relationships as enhancing personal intimacy. The intolerance of homosexual expression by the official Church teaching or by a May and a Grisez is due, in part, because they see it as hedonistic self-indulgence promoting an illusory human intimacy.

One of the problems with human intimacy, as Andrew Greeley has pointed out, indeed the most basic problem, is what intimacy does to human beings. Intimacy has a warm and comfortable sound, connoting safety, peace, and completeness. Yet intimacy "releases forces in our personalities that we do not understand and can only imperfectly control."[10] An intimate relationship intensifies our capacity to love, but also our capacity to hate. It brings intense joy, but also intense sorrow. It has a profound transforming power which is both its promise and its peril. And it constitutes for most human beings the school in which they will learn or fail to learn the meaning of God's love for them.

The quest for intimacy takes place in a context of human sinfulness in which love for the other struggles with lust. As John Paul II explained:

The lust of the flesh [is] a permanent element of man's sinfulness (*status naturae lapsae*). The lust which, as an interior act, springs from this basis ... damages the very intentionality of the woman's existence for man, reducing the riches of the perennial call to the communion of per-

sons, the riches of the deep attractiveness of masculinity
and femininity to mere satisfaction of the sexual need of the
body.[11]

The human fear of intimacy and the ever present possibility of lust
threaten to turn the sexual dynamic toward intimacy and personal
communion into the impersonal satisfaction of sexual desire. The
twofold task, then, of sexual morality is to guard against lust, but
also to promote intimacy.

4. The Social Importance of Sexuality

That human sexuality has social significance is not a new discovery. The manifest importance of procreation for the survival of
the human species is too obvious to need mention. But several features of the contemporary world have conspired to turn sexuality
and sexual expression into a private matter, with the result that culturally and legally what two—or more—consenting adults do in the
privacy of their home is thought to be of no concern to society. The
most graphic sign of this development is the repeal of laws concerning adultery, fornication, homosexual acts and the sale of contraceptives. No-fault divorce laws are another indication. Society appears
less and less interested in stable marriages and more and more tolerant of any form of sexual expression. Only rape and child molesta-
tion are matters of social concern, and, then, only as a protection of
individual rights.

But there is a consensus among all the moralists in the Catholic
tradition that, despite the changes in the contemporary world, human sexuality remains a profoundly social reality with great importance for the well-being of society. Human sexual expression, to be
authentically human, must be socially responsible, to use the term of
Human Sexuality. Again, while disputes continue over the precise
implications of this requirement, it is not a trivial point of agreement
and sets their understanding of sexual morality at odds with most of
the secular culture. The two most obvious issues of social concern
are the issues of divorce and remarriage and birth control. The civil
rights of homosexuals, while certainly of social concern, are a matter

of justice, not sexual morality. Abortion, also a pressing social concern, is not an issue in sexual morality but in the ethics of killing.

Earlier it was suggested that it is the dynamic of personal intimacy itself that raises the demand for fruitfulness, or it is the very nature of human sexual love to be life-giving. Now that being fruitful and multiplying is more of a human problem than a human need, this claim about the nature of sexual love requires careful consideration. The sexual dynamic toward intimacy leads people to a shared life. For there to be a shared life, there must be life to share. The life in question is not primarily the life of a child. It is one another's life. The sharing unique to sexual intimacy is not the sharing of a common interest, or a common job, or a common hobby, although such sharing can be an important help to personal intimacy. The sharing unique to sexual intimacy is the total sharing of self, quaintly called the sharing of bed and board. This sharing, this mutual love, when placed in the Christian context of belief, contains in itself the demand to be life-giving. Or as John Paul told an Irish audience, "God himself, who created male and female . . . created them in his own image, reflecting his own life-giving love in the patterns of their sexual being."[12]

It is important to note that the Pope does not say that God's own life-giving love is reflected in the pattern of their sexual organs but of their sexual being. It is their mutual personal love, if authentic, that reaches out to share itself more widely even while preserving its own intimate dynamic. A useful analogy may be drawn here between the love of the couple and the love of God in Christ as received by the Church. The hearing of the good news of God's love in Christ is not, and cannot be kept, a private matter. It must be proclaimed, shared with others. As the First Epistle of John states the matter, "What we have seen and heard we are telling you so that you too may be in union with us, as we are in union with the Father and with his Son Jesus Christ. We are writing this to you to make our own joy complete" (1 Jn 1:3–4). In a similar way, the mutual love of the couple demands to be shared, and, where possible, in the creation of new life. The family is born; children are invited to share in the life and love of their parents.

This orientation of sexual love to the creation of new life is a matter of common consensus among all the authors studied here. For sexual love to be authentically love and fully human it must have such an orientation. It is the implications of this that are still disputed, and that need, and no doubt will receive, further clarification in the future development of sexual morality. It may be that the case for natural family planning will be able to show more clearly both its universal effectiveness as a method of birth control and its essential relatedness to human dignity, so that artificial means of contraception would constitute not only an ontic evil, but also a moral evil. However, it is hard to see, at least for this author, that such a case has been made.

The family is the primary social unit of society. While it has lost many of its historical functions over the years, it remains the primary instrument of early socialization and the prime source of emotional fulfillment for adults. The stability and well-being of the family, and so also of marriage, has important personal and social consequences. This is readily attested to by the number of unwanted pregnancies, the drug problem, the amount of juvenile crime and rootlessness, the tragic emotional consequences of divorce, and so on. The doctrine on the indissolubility of marriage and the prohibition of remarriage to a third party after divorce, while having their bases in Scripture and the traditional understanding of the marital bond, also serve the purpose of a stable marriage and family. Unfortunately, they may or may not serve the well-being of the marriage and the family. Pastorally, it is no longer common to urge parents to stay together for the sake of the children when the marriage has broken down to the point where the home is a place of acrimony and emotional tension and insecurity. Marriages do seem to break down, with regrettably increasing frequency. Should remarriage be permitted or is it always morally wrong?

That marriage ought to be indissoluble, that in marrying a couple create a moral bond that should be dissolved only by death, is also a matter of consensus among Christian theologians. So much is this the case that evidence that one or both of the marriage partners had reservations about or put conditions on the permanency of the commitment is grounds for annulment. So, also, is evidence that one or both partners lacked the maturity or the freedom to make a per-

manent commitment. But is it, and why is it always morally wrong
to attempt a second marriage after a divorce? This is the question
that is debated,[13] along with the concern that a change in the
Church's teaching would further weaken the ideal of indissolubility
and the stability of marriage. Such a concern is clearly evident, for
example, in Charles Curran's carefully nuanced argument for a
change in the teaching on indissolubility.[14] Even while advocating
the change, Curran urges that the real task is to "expend every effort
possible to strengthen the loving marriage commitment of spouses,
even if the eschatological ideal cannot always be fulfilled in our present and limited world."[15]

The question of divorce and remarriage is debated more properly in sacramental theology, but an ethical approach might ask whether the teaching itself is not inhumane and cruel. That marriage is
understood to be a sacrament, on an analogy with baptism, confirmation, holy orders, the Eucharist, and so on, complicates and even
confuses the issue. For sacraments cannot be undone. Once a person
is baptized or confirmed, he or she can fail to live up to the obligations of the sacrament, but not be unbaptized or unconfirmed. Once
consecrated, the Eucharist is the body and blood of Christ. It cannot
be returned to bread and wine. Once ordained, a priest is a priest forever. While he may be relieved of the Church-imposed obligations of
celibacy and saying the office, he is not excused of the obligation of
administering the sacraments of reconciliation and the anointing of
the sick when there is urgent pastoral need and no other priest is
available. How can the married be unmarried?

Karl Barth, the renowned German reformed theologian, once
accused Catholics of having a theology of the wedding but not a theology of marriage. It is not the wedding, as Bishop Francis Stafford
has reminded us, but the whole marriage that is the sacrament,[16]
which makes it considerably different than other sacraments. If the
sacramental bond is understood to be a moral bond, then it can be
broken, though never without sin. The sin involved, however, cannot
be understood as a single act or a series of acts. It would more likely
be a pattern of indifference or insensitivity or neglect. In such a case,
the sin could be sincerely repented for, even while acknowledging the
marriage bond to be destroyed and the marriage dead. Paul Ramsey

has shown how Eastern Orthodoxy has dealt with this possibility both canonically and liturgically without imperiling the Church's witness to the indissolubility of Christian marriage.[17] His is a suggestion that deserves to be pursued in this age of ecumenical theology.

5. Sex as Ritual

In concluding this study of what they are saying about sexual morality, one final suggestion might also point to a future direction. James Burtchaell has made the proposal that sex is a ritual activity and is best understood in that way.[18] That means, of course, that we need to have some understanding of what ritual is and what its purpose is. The rituals that most people are familiar with in our culture are religious or patriotic ones. Churchgoers are familiar with the Sunday rituals of their worship. Citizens are acquainted with the rituals that surround holidays such as July 4, Memorial Day or Thanksgiving, and special occasions such as the inauguration of a president or the honoring of returned astronauts.

All rituals, but, perhaps, religious rituals most of all, risk three dangers—the dangers of hypocrisy, boredom and magic. Because ritual activity is public activity and carried out in the presence of others,' there is the constant temptation to show off, to play to the crowd, to use the ritual for one's own sake rather than for the purposes for which it is intended. All churches know that hypocrisy is the great spoiler of worship, and youth are often particularly sensitive to it, often believing that adults are in church not to worship God but to be seen by other adults. Accordingly the ritual is rejected as so much empty show.

This danger also besets sex as a ritual of love when the words of love are without true intent and substance, and sex is used simply as a means of self-gratification or sexual release. Especially people who are hurt or disappointed in love affairs, or who are cynical about the very possibility of human love, find the ritual of sex to be so much empty show. Since sex cannot be dismissed as easily as Sunday church attendance, a repressive or manipulative approach to one's sexuality is taken. But in either case, sex as a ritual of love remains empty.

A second danger that ritual runs is that of boredom. This danger has two causes which are closely related. Ritual acts are repetitive. Every Sunday, with minor exceptions, we go through the same routine, so that to some people it becomes a deadly formality or a meaningless and repetitive game of no substance. They want something new, something relevant. Rituals can also be done badly, carried out in such a way that it becomes positively distasteful. The music is so terrible, the sermon so banal, the reading of liturgical texts so garbled that the best one can do is withdraw into oneself and suffer in silence.

This same danger besets sex. Sexual actions are repetitive. The same kisses, the same caresses, the same act of intercourse, the same release, and so to sleep. Being creatures of habit, people fall into patterns. And sex becomes boring, a deadly formality of a relationship. So people look for something new, something with more spice to it—a new partner, perhaps, or group sex, or a new position, but with repetition these, too, pale and the search for the new continues. Or sex can be badly done, as Dr. Reuben and Masters and Johnson and Alex Comfort and other sex manualists have discovered to their profit. Men can be so inept at love-making that the best a woman is able to do is suffer in silence. Women can be so inept or so unresponsive that the man simply loses interest. The ritual is simply a bore. Just as it is possible to decide that one gets more out of worshiping alone, so, too, one decides that solitary sex leads to better results.

The third danger that imperils ritual is that of magic, and this happens as a consequence of a fundamental misunderstanding, or, more accurately, two misunderstandings. As Burtchaell explains it in regard to religion:

> It has ever been a temptation for Christians to consider ethics as a means of changing God; by proper behavior one would win the divine favor. The same temptation is endemic to worship: men would use it to turn God's head, to abate his wrath. . . . The second misunderstanding is that the disciplined and energetic conduct whereby one grows to be a loving man can somehow be replaced by worship. It is this twofold twist—that worship can manipulate God, and obviates ethics—which makes for magic.[19]

Sex, a ritual of love, does not escape this twofold twist. There are those people who believe that sex will make the other person love them, conform to their wishes and desires, and meet their needs. There are people who believe that sex can manipulate the object of their affection and desire. Of course, in some cases this is exactly the case, but then sex is, indeed, a magical means to gain control and domination. It is hardly a fully human expression of love. There are also people who believe that sex can be substituted for love. In place of the acts of service, understanding, support, forgiveness, and fidelity which mark one as loving, they attempt to put sexual acts. The meaning of loving becomes having sex, as is the case in the popular culture. This has its classic illustration in the man who tells a woman that, if she loved him, she would go to bed with him, when, in fact, the very opposite is the case.

Those, however, are merely the dangers that befall ritual. Despite these dangers ritual remains a deep human need and a powerful, shaping experience. Despite its routine character, ritual is the antidote to routine. It is the occasion on which the daily routine is halted and the meaning of our daily lives is focused and celebrated. Ritual is necessary for human beings lest they lose sight of the meaning of their lives and become worn down by the daily tasks they perform. Human beings need parties, parades and public worship.

Ritual also has a powerful shaping effect on human beings. Not only does it focus and celebrate the meaning of our own lives in some particular way. It actually reinforces and enhances that meaning. When, for example, students who are friends have a party to celebrate the successful completion of a school year, the party itself is a deepening of their friendship and an impetus to continue seeking the education they jointly pursue. Why do we need ritual and why must that ritual be compatible with the occasion we celebrate?

> Because it is through ritual that we bring purpose to our lives. Our rituals provide us with intense moments of meaning, opportunities to display the powerfully operative forces that shape the way we live. It is by ritual that we embody why we live and celebrate what we believe. Ritual releases meaning. Better put—it craves meaning, and can possess it

only from other kinds of human activity. It cannot supply meaning, it only reveals it.[20]

As a ritual act, sex cannot supply or reveal a meaning to a relationship that is not already present. If there is nothing to celebrate in the relationship, sex is a fraud, inauthentic, immoral. But of what is the fullness of sexual expression a ritual? It cannot be a ritual simply of love, for we have many loves—father, mother, brothers, sisters, friends—which we ritually celebrate on birthdays and holidays without sexual intercourse being a factor. Rather sexual intercourse is a ritual of a fully shared life that is open to the world and to the future. It can counterfeit itself as something else, but then it succumbs to the dangers of ritual and is inauthentic human behavior.

The Christian sexual vision is a high one, an ideal of which we all fall short at times. Every failure should not be seen as a serious lapse, or, in traditional terms, as a mortal sin. Whether this is interpreted in terms of its impact on one's fundamental option or in terms of the diminishment of subjective culpability, not all falling short of the ideal is grievously evil. But every failure to live one's sexuality authentically and humanly can serve as a serious question to one's conscience to ask what he or she is really thinking about sexual morality and whether a serious change of mind and heart is called for. Sexual morality is no longer being seen as a restraint on sexuality, but as a developing guide to authentic human personhood and to communities of life and love we call the family.

In sum, what they are saying about human sexuality stresses the goodness and the promise of committed sexual relationships as a primary place for human growth, both personal and social. Increasingly Christian sexual morality finds itself at odds with the morality of the secular culture which denies the free and rational control of the sexual instinct as a primary moral task. At the same time a more compassionate pastoral concern has joined hands with moral theology to seek new answers to the dilemmas created by failed marriages, homosexuality, and the growing urgency of responsible parenthood. Most clear of all the developments is the recognition that human beings were not made for sex, but sex was made for human beings. It is God's gift to increase our love both for one another and for him.

Only to the extent that it genuinely does this can we talk about a healthy sexual morality.

Notes

1. R. May, pp. 181–241, 275–286.

2. McBrien, p. 13.

3. See *Origins* 9, No. 20 (Nov. 1, 1979), p. 325; *Origins* 10, No. 1 (May 22, 1980), pp. 260–262; *Origins* 10, No. 18 (October 16, 1980), p. 286, for some representative indications of their views.

4. For the possible relationships of moral rules to love see Regan, pp. 102–112.

5. For the terms and a similar analysis of them, but in a different context, see Hannah Arendt, *The Human Condition* (Chicago: University of Chicago Press, 1958), pp. 79–247; Grisez and Shaw, pp. 1–30, talk of three levels of action.

6. For a useful introduction to this whole question see Daniel C. Maguire, "*Human Sexuality*: The Book and the Epiphenomenon," *Proceedings of the Catholic Theological Society of America* 33 (1978), pp. 66–68.

7. See the Congregation's evaluation of the book *Human Sexuality* in *Origins* 9, No. 11 (Aug. 30, 1979), p. 168, and Murphy, p. 45.

8. Greeley, p. 144; he explores this question more fully in Andrew M. Greeley, *Sexual Intimacy* (Chicago: Thomas More Press, 1973).

9. Overberg, pp. 70–72.

10. Greeley, *The New Agenda*, p. 155.

11. Pope John Paul II, "Lust and Personal Dignity," *Origins* 10, No. 19 (Oct. 23, 1980), p. 303.

12. *Ibid.*, "Homily in County Limerick," *Origins* 9, No. 20 (Nov. 1, 1977), p. 325.

13. A useful example of the debate can be found in Mary Durkin and James Hitchcock, *Catholic Perspectives: Divorce* (Chicago: The Thomas More Press, 1979).

14. Charles E. Curran, "Divorce in the Light of a Revised Mor-